All About Louvre: A Kid's Guide to Paris' Most Famous Museum

Educational Books For Kids, Volume 21

Shah Rukh

Published by Shah Rukh, 2024.

While every precaution has been taken in the preparation of this book, the publisher assumes no responsibility for errors or omissions, or for damages resulting from the use of the information contained herein.

ALL ABOUT LOUVRE: A KID'S GUIDE TO PARIS' MOST FAMOUS MUSEUM

First edition. September 27, 2024.

Copyright © 2024 Shah Rukh.

ISBN: 979-8224209569

Written by Shah Rukh.

Table of Contents

Prologue

Welcome to the Louvre, one of the most magical places on Earth! Nestled in the heart of Paris, the Louvre Museum is not just any museum – it's the largest art museum in the world, and it holds some of the greatest treasures from history. From ancient mummies and golden crowns to famous paintings like the *Mona Lisa*, there's so much to explore and discover.

But the Louvre wasn't always a museum. It started as a grand palace for kings and queens, filled with secret chambers, massive towers, and incredible artwork. Over the centuries, it transformed into the museum we know today, welcoming millions of visitors every year who come to marvel at its wonders.

In this book, you'll take an exciting journey through the Louvre's rich history, uncovering its hidden gems and learning about the fascinating stories behind its most famous exhibits. Whether you're an art lover or just curious about the world, there's something for everyone here.

So, grab your explorer's hat, and let's dive into the adventure of a lifetime, right inside the walls of the Louvre!

Chapter 1: The Origins of the Louvre

The origins of the Louvre trace back over 800 years, making it one of the oldest and most historically significant buildings in Paris. What began as a medieval fortress during the reign of King Philippe Auguste in the late 12th century has evolved into the world's most famous art museum. Philippe Auguste, concerned about the safety of Paris while he was away on the Crusades, commissioned the construction of a large defensive fortress on the city's outskirts to protect it from invasions. This structure, completed around 1202, was initially designed to shield the western approach to Paris from potential attacks, especially those coming from the English, who were then significant rivals.

At that time, the Louvre was far from the magnificent palace it would eventually become. It was a dark, imposing fortress with high walls, a deep moat, and a massive keep, or "donjon," at its center, designed to hold a garrison of soldiers. The layout was square, with towers on each corner, and was strategically located along the Seine River, which made it a critical point of defense. This early version of the Louvre was a place of military strength rather than artistic or cultural significance, meant to ensure the safety of the monarchy and the people of Paris.

As Paris grew and flourished during the Renaissance, so too did the Louvre. By the 16th century, under the rule of King François I, the fortress began to transform into a royal residence. François, who was an avid art collector and a significant patron of the arts, invited artists, including the famous Leonardo da Vinci, to his court. François' passion for art and culture helped lay the groundwork for the Louvre's eventual role as a center of artistic display. It was François who initiated the demolition of the medieval fortress, replacing it with a Renaissance-style palace. He also started expanding the Louvre's collection by acquiring works of art, including the Mona Lisa, which he purchased from Leonardo himself.

However, it wasn't just François I who left his mark on the Louvre. Successive French kings continued to transform the building into an opulent palace. Henry II, Charles IX, and Henry IV all contributed to the ongoing construction projects at the Louvre, enlarging it and giving it a more lavish, palace-like appearance. Perhaps the most significant contribution came from King Louis XIV, known as the Sun King, who undertook grand projects at the Louvre, although he eventually shifted his court to the Palace of Versailles. Under Louis XIV, the Louvre ceased to be the primary royal residence, yet the building's transformation into a masterpiece of architecture and art continued. By this time, the Louvre was no longer a military fortress but a symbol of royal power, wealth, and artistic taste.

The most dramatic change in the Louvre's history came in 1793, during the French Revolution. The monarchy was overthrown, and the Louvre, which had served as a royal residence for centuries, was turned into a public museum. The revolutionary government declared that the magnificent art collection amassed by generations of French kings would now belong to the people. On August 10, 1793, the Louvre opened its doors as a museum for the first time, marking the beginning of a new chapter in its long history. This opening, which took place on the anniversary of the fall of the monarchy, symbolized a shift in the way art and culture were perceived in society. No longer the exclusive domain of royalty and the elite, the treasures of the Louvre were now accessible to ordinary citizens.

The early days of the Louvre as a museum were not without challenges. Many of the original art collections had been damaged or dispersed during the Revolution. The museum itself was in a state of disrepair after years of neglect. However, efforts to restore the building and its collections were soon underway, and over the following decades, the Louvre grew into the world-renowned institution it is today. Under Napoleon Bonaparte, the museum was greatly expanded, and its collections grew thanks to the spoils of war. Napoleon, who renamed the museum the "Musée Napoléon," brought back a wealth of art from his military campaigns across Europe, including pieces from Italy, Egypt, and the Netherlands. Although many of these works were later returned to their countries of origin after his defeat, Napoleon's contributions to the Louvre's collection were substantial.

Throughout the 19th and 20th centuries, the Louvre continued to expand, both in terms of its physical size and the scope of its collection. New wings were added, and galleries were built to house the growing number of artworks, artifacts, and antiquities. In 1989, the Louvre underwent one of its most controversial and well-known transformations with the addition of the glass pyramid designed by architect I. M. Pei. This modern structure, placed in the Louvre's courtyard, became an iconic symbol of the museum, blending contemporary architecture with the historic surroundings.

Today, the Louvre is a testament to the evolution of French history and culture. It houses over 35,000 works of art, spanning from ancient civilizations to the 19th century. The museum's collection includes some of the most famous works of art in the world, such as the Mona Lisa, the Venus de Milo, and the Winged Victory of Samothrace. It is not only a museum but a symbol of Paris itself, drawing millions of visitors each year from across the globe.

The Louvre's origins as a fortress, its transformation into a royal palace, and its ultimate destiny as the world's largest and most visited museum reflect the changing nature of French society and politics over the centuries. What began as a symbol of military power and royal wealth has become a cultural treasure open to all, showcasing the creativity and artistic achievements of humanity across time. The Louvre's journey from a defensive stronghold to a global center of art and culture is a fascinating testament to its enduring importance in the history of France and the world.

Chapter 2: The Louvre's Transformation from Palace to Museum

The transformation of the Louvre from a royal palace into the world's largest and most famous museum is a story of immense cultural, political, and architectural evolution. It spans several centuries, reflecting the shifting power dynamics, artistic tastes, and societal changes in France. This remarkable journey from a grand seat of royal power to a cultural institution accessible to the public mirrors the history of France itself, particularly its transition from monarchy to republic. The Louvre's metamorphosis is one of the most intriguing examples of how spaces can change roles dramatically over time while preserving layers of history within their walls.

The Louvre's story as a palace began in the 12th century when King Philippe Auguste built a fortress to protect Paris from potential invaders. The early Louvre was not a palace as we think of it today; it was a military stronghold, intended to guard the city from the west and protect the monarchy. The massive fortress, with its deep moat and towering walls, served as a visual reminder of royal power and control. Over time, as the medieval fortress stood firm against threats, it became increasingly evident that the Louvre's role could evolve beyond mere defense.

By the 16th century, during the Renaissance, French kings began to view the Louvre as a potential royal residence. King François I, a monarch with a deep love of art and culture, initiated the Louvre's first major transformation. He ordered the demolition of the old medieval fortress to make way for a Renaissance-style palace that would reflect the growing sophistication and power of the French monarchy. François I's ambition to create a magnificent royal residence coincided with his efforts to make France a hub of art and culture. Under his reign, artists like Leonardo da Vinci were invited to France, and

François began amassing a collection of artworks that would one day form the core of the Louvre's Museum collection.

As subsequent kings continued to build upon François I's vision, the Louvre became a symbol of royal luxury and splendor. Henry II, Charles IX, and Henry IV all added their own expansions to the palace, turning it into a sprawling complex of wings, courtyards, and galleries. During the reign of Louis XIII and Louis XIV, the Louvre became an even grander residence, with monumental architectural projects such as the construction of the Pavillon de l'Horloge and the Grande Galerie. However, as Louis XIV's reign progressed, his focus shifted away from the Louvre, and he chose to move his court to the more opulent Palace of Versailles. Versailles, with its vast gardens and lavish rooms, became the new symbol of royal power, and the Louvre began to be used less frequently as a residence.

Despite Louis XIV's relocation of the royal court, the Louvre's evolution continued. Even as it ceased to be the primary royal residence, its grandeur and architectural development persisted. The palace housed various government offices and royal academies, becoming a focal point for cultural institutions like the Académie des Beaux-Arts. In this period, the Louvre's galleries began to be filled with artistic works, many of which were the personal collections of the kings of France. Although the palace was not yet open to the public, its role as a repository of art and culture was growing. The seeds of its eventual transformation into a museum had been planted, even though they wouldn't fully blossom until after the French Revolution.

The most pivotal moment in the Louvre's transformation came in 1789 with the outbreak of the French Revolution. The revolution, which overthrew the monarchy and dramatically reshaped French society, also redefined the role of the Louvre. As the revolutionaries sought to dismantle the symbols of royal power and privilege, they looked for ways to repurpose the nation's grandest institutions. The Louvre, with its vast collections of royal art, was an obvious candidate for change. Instead of remaining a symbol of monarchy and exclusivity, it was decided that the Louvre should be transformed into a museum open to the public. This decision was both practical and ideological; by opening the Louvre's doors to ordinary citizens, the revolutionary government sought to demonstrate the new ideals of equality and access to culture.

In 1793, just four years after the Revolution began, the Louvre officially opened its doors as a museum. This event marked a revolutionary moment not only for France but for the world of art. For the first time, the royal collections that had been amassed over centuries were available for public viewing. Art that had once been the exclusive property of kings and nobility was now part of the collective cultural heritage of the French people. The initial opening featured a modest collection of around 500 works, many of which had been seized from the aristocracy or the Catholic Church during the revolution. The museum's creation reflected the changing notions of ownership and access to cultural treasures, reinforcing the idea that art belonged to the people rather than a select few.

The Louvre's early years as a museum were not without difficulties. The building itself had suffered from neglect during the revolutionary turmoil, and many of the artworks were in a state of disrepair. Furthermore, the collections were relatively small compared to what the Louvre would eventually hold. Nonetheless, the museum quickly became a focal point of Parisian life, and over time, its collection grew. Napoleon Bonaparte played a significant role in expanding the museum during his reign. He ordered the acquisition and display of countless artworks, many of which were taken from his military conquests across Europe. Napoleon even renamed the museum the "Musée Napoléon," and under his leadership, the Louvre became a symbol of French imperial power as well as a showcase of the artistic treasures of Europe. Although many of these artworks were later returned to their countries of origin following Napoleon's defeat, his contributions to the Louvre's expansion were significant.

As the 19th century progressed, the Louvre's role as a museum became firmly established. Successive French governments continued to support the expansion of the museum's collections and its physical space. Under the reigns of Louis XVIII and Charles X, and during the July Monarchy of Louis-Philippe, the museum grew significantly. New wings were added, including the famous Galerie d'Apollon, and the collections expanded to include not only paintings but also sculptures, decorative arts, and antiquities. The Louvre was no longer just a place to view the treasures of the French monarchy but had become a comprehensive museum showcasing the art and culture of civilizations from around the world.

In the 20th century, the Louvre underwent another major transformation with the introduction of modern elements to the historic site. Perhaps the most iconic of these changes was the addition of the glass pyramid in the central courtyard, designed by the architect I. M. Pei and completed in 1989. The pyramid, which serves as the main entrance to the museum, sparked controversy when it was first unveiled. Many Parisians and art lovers were critical of placing a modern, minimalist structure in the heart of such a historically significant site. However, over time, the pyramid became an iconic symbol of the Louvre itself, representing the museum's ability to blend its rich historical past with contemporary architectural innovation.

Today, the Louvre is a global cultural institution, housing over 35,000 works of art that span from ancient civilizations to the 19th century. Its collections include some of the most famous and valuable artworks in the world, such as Leonardo da Vinci's *Mona Lisa*, the *Venus de Milo*, and the *Winged Victory of Samothrace*. The museum attracts over 10 million visitors each year, making it the most visited museum in the world. While the Louvre's origins as a fortress and royal palace are still visible in its architecture and layout, its transformation into a public museum is a testament to the power of art and culture to transcend politics and history.

The Louvre's journey from a royal palace to a museum reflects broader shifts in French society and the world at large. It is a story of how spaces can be repurposed to serve new ideals, how art can move from the private to the public sphere, and how cultural institutions evolve to meet the needs of changing societies. The Louvre's transformation is not just the story of a building; it is the story of France's transformation from monarchy to republic, from exclusivity to accessibility, and from national treasure to global icon.

Chapter 3: Exploring the Louvre's Glass Pyramid

Exploring the Louvre's glass pyramid is an iconic experience for visitors to Paris and a defining feature of the world's most famous museum. The pyramid, designed by Chinese-American architect I. M. Pei, stands in stark contrast to the historical grandeur of the Louvre's classical architecture. Its sleek, modern design made it a subject of intense debate and controversy when it was first unveiled in 1989. Today, however, it is celebrated as a symbol of the museum's fusion of history and modernity, becoming one of the most recognized architectural landmarks in the world. The story behind the pyramid, its conception, design, and the role it plays in the Louvre's function, is a fascinating exploration into how architecture can shape the identity of a cultural institution.

Before the pyramid was conceived, the Louvre had been struggling with issues related to the sheer number of visitors it received each year. By the late 20th century, the museum had become a sprawling maze of galleries, corridors, and courtyards. Its labyrinthine structure, the result of centuries of additions and renovations, made navigation challenging for visitors. Entry to the museum was through the original doors of the palace, which were not designed to accommodate the millions of people who flocked to see the Louvre's extensive collections. This led to long lines, overcrowding, and logistical difficulties, detracting from the overall visitor experience. The need for a new entrance that could handle the flow of tourists while maintaining the integrity of the museum's historical character became evident.

In 1981, then-French President François Mitterrand announced the Grand Louvre project, an ambitious plan to renovate and expand the museum. One of the primary goals of the project was to create a new central entrance that would provide a better experience for the growing number of visitors. Mitterrand turned to architect I. M. Pei, who had already earned international recognition for his work on projects like the East Building of the National Gallery of Art in Washington, D.C., and the John F. Kennedy Library in Boston. Pei's reputation for blending modern architectural elements with historical environments made him a suitable choice for such a prestigious project. However, the design he proposed—a glass pyramid—was met with considerable resistance and skepticism from both the public and architectural critics.

Pei's glass pyramid was a radical departure from the traditional aesthetic of the Louvre. The museum, with its roots in medieval fortresses and royal palaces, had long been a symbol of classical architecture. Its façades, adorned with ornate sculptures, colonnades, and grand windows, exuded the grandeur of French royalty and empire. Against this backdrop, the idea of installing a minimalist, geometric structure made entirely of glass and metal in the heart of the Cour Napoléon was seen as jarring. Many critics argued that the pyramid would clash with the historic integrity of the Louvre, accusing Pei of designing a structure that would look more at home in a modern business district than in the courtyard of a centuries-old palace. Some likened it to an "inverted spaceship," and others feared it would permanently ruin the aesthetic balance of the museum.

Despite the criticism, Pei stood by his vision. He argued that the pyramid, though modern in its design, would harmonize with the existing Louvre architecture in both form and function. The pyramid's proportions, Pei explained, echoed the classical symmetry of the Louvre's buildings, while its transparent glass allowed the structure to complement, rather than overpower, the surrounding architecture. The pyramid's simple geometric form was intended to serve as a focal point, drawing visitors toward the museum's entrance and organizing the space in a way that would make navigation more intuitive. Additionally, the use of glass symbolized transparency and openness, values that Pei believed were central to the Louvre's mission as a public institution. Rather than imposing a new architectural style onto the museum, Pei sought to create a structure that would enhance the visitor experience while respecting the Louvre's historical significance.

One of the pyramid's most remarkable features is its material: glass. Pei's use of glass was not just a modern aesthetic choice; it was also a technical challenge. The pyramid is composed of 673 individual panes of glass arranged in a precise geometric pattern. Contrary to an urban legend that the pyramid contains exactly 666 panes—a number with symbolic significance in various religious traditions—the actual number is higher, ensuring both the structural integrity and the visual elegance of the design. Each pane was meticulously crafted to minimize reflections and distortions, allowing visitors to see the Louvre's surrounding buildings clearly through the glass. This transparency, combined with the pyramid's minimalist frame, creates the illusion that the structure is lighter than air, blending seamlessly into the environment despite its modernity.

The pyramid stands 21.6 meters (71 feet) tall and has a square base measuring 35.4 meters (116 feet) on each side. These dimensions were carefully calculated to maintain a balance with the surrounding architecture. The pyramid's structure was designed not only as an architectural statement but also to serve a practical purpose: to serve as the new main entrance to the Louvre, capable of accommodating millions of visitors each year. Beneath the pyramid lies an expansive underground lobby, which connects to various wings of the museum. This design revolutionized the way visitors experience the Louvre. Instead of entering through one of the palace's smaller doors and navigating its maze-like layout, visitors are now funneled through the spacious lobby, where they can access the different wings of the museum with ease.

One of the pyramid's most ingenious aspects is its role in solving the logistical problems that had plagued the Louvre for years. The underground lobby not only serves as an entry point but also houses ticketing areas, information desks, and other visitor services, which helps to streamline the flow of traffic. From this central hub, visitors can ascend into the museum's various galleries, including the Denon, Richelieu, and Sully wings, which house famous artworks such as the *Mona Lisa*, the *Venus de Milo*, and the *Winged Victory of Samothrace*. By placing the main entrance underground, Pei was able to preserve the historic exterior of the Louvre while enhancing the functionality of the museum. The glass pyramid serves as a visual and architectural centerpiece, guiding visitors naturally toward the entrance while also symbolizing the museum's embrace of both tradition and modernity.

Despite the initial controversy, the glass pyramid quickly became an iconic symbol of the Louvre and, by extension, of Paris itself. Over the years, it has come to be seen as a triumph of modern architecture, proving that contemporary design can coexist harmoniously with historic structures. The pyramid's success lies in its ability to connect the past with the present. It is a reminder that even institutions as old as the Louvre must adapt to the needs of a changing world, yet they can do so in a way that enhances their timeless beauty rather than diminishing it. The pyramid's glass walls reflect not only the grandeur of the Louvre's architecture but also the thousands of visitors who pass through its entrance every day, symbolizing the ongoing relationship between the museum and the public it serves.

In addition to the main pyramid, Pei's design includes three smaller pyramids that surround the central structure. These smaller pyramids provide additional sources of natural light for the underground lobby and create a sense of balance in the overall design. The courtyard itself was reimagined as a space that invites exploration and reflection, with fountains and open spaces where visitors can pause and admire the surrounding architecture. The combination of these elements—light, water, glass, and stone—creates a dynamic environment that changes with the time of day and the seasons, making each visit to the Louvre unique.

Over time, the glass pyramid has become a beloved symbol of the Louvre, appearing in countless photographs, films, and works of art. It has been the backdrop for cultural events, celebrations, and even protests, becoming a space where art, history, and contemporary life intersect. In popular culture, the pyramid gained international fame when it was featured in Dan Brown's bestselling novel *The Da Vinci Code*, further cementing its place in the public imagination. The pyramid's distinctive silhouette has made it one of the most recognizable features of the Parisian skyline, alongside landmarks like the Eiffel Tower and Notre-Dame Cathedral.

The pyramid's success also sparked a broader conversation about the role of modern architecture in historic environments. Pei's design demonstrated that it is possible to introduce contemporary elements into a heritage site without compromising its integrity. This approach has since been emulated in other cultural institutions around the world, from the British Museum in London to the Museum of Modern Art in New York. The Louvre's glass pyramid stands as a testament to the idea that history and modernity can coexist, enhancing each other rather than standing in opposition.

Today, exploring the Louvre's glass pyramid is an essential part of any visit to the museum. For many, it serves as the first point of contact with the Louvre, offering a striking introduction to the wonders that lie within. As visitors pass through its transparent walls, they enter a space where centuries of history, art, and culture converge. The pyramid not only guides visitors into the heart of the museum but also serves as a reminder of the Louvre's ongoing evolution. It represents the museum's commitment to preserving its past while embracing the future, ensuring that the Louvre remains a living, dynamic institution for generations to come.

The glass pyramid has transformed the Louvre from a stately palace of the past into a vibrant cultural landmark of the present and future. Its ability to blend cutting-edge design with historical reverence makes it a powerful symbol of innovation and tradition.

15

Chapter 4: Masterpieces Inside the Louvre

The Louvre, as the world's largest and most visited museum, is home to thousands of priceless works of art spanning several millennia. Its extensive collection encompasses everything from ancient artifacts and classical sculptures to Renaissance masterpieces and modern treasures. With over 35,000 works of art on display, the Louvre's collection is an unparalleled reflection of humanity's artistic achievements. However, certain pieces stand out, both for their artistic merit and the historical or cultural significance they carry. These masterpieces have become synonymous with the Louvre itself, drawing millions of visitors from around the globe to marvel at their beauty and craftsmanship. In this exploration of the most renowned masterpieces inside the Louvre, we will delve into the history, artistry, and impact of these iconic works, offering a glimpse into the museum's unparalleled collection.

Arguably the most famous piece in the Louvre, and perhaps the most famous painting in the world, is Leonardo da Vinci's *Mona Lisa*. Housed in a room specifically dedicated to it, the *Mona Lisa* has become a symbol of art and mystery, captivating visitors with its enigmatic smile. Painted in the early 16th century, the *Mona Lisa* was commissioned by a wealthy Florentine merchant, and it is widely believed to be a portrait of his wife, Lisa Gherardini. The painting's fame is due to several factors, not the least of which is da Vinci's revolutionary technique. Leonardo's use of sfumato, a method that creates soft transitions between colors and tones, gives the *Mona Lisa* her lifelike quality and an aura of ethereal mystery. The play of light and shadow on her face, combined with the serene, yet inscrutable expression, has fascinated viewers for centuries. Furthermore, the *Mona Lisa* became a worldwide sensation after it was stolen from the Louvre in 1911 and recovered two years later. Its theft and subsequent recovery only added to its mythos, cementing its status as a cultural icon. Today, despite the relatively small size of the painting, the *Mona Lisa* is protected behind bulletproof glass and is constantly surrounded by crowds of visitors, all eager to catch a glimpse of the famous smile.

Another of the Louvre's masterpieces is *The Raft of the Medusa*, painted by Théodore Géricault in 1819. This massive painting, which measures over 16 feet in width, depicts a harrowing real-life event: the wreck of the French naval frigate *Medusa* off the coast of Senegal in 1816. The ship's captain and officers, who were politically appointed and grossly incompetent, abandoned the crew and passengers on a makeshift raft. After two weeks at sea, only a handful of survivors remained, enduring starvation, exposure, and even cannibalism. Géricault's painting captures the moment when the survivors spot a ship on the horizon, their hopes for rescue tempered by their horrific ordeal. The painting is notable for its dramatic composition, with figures in various states of despair and desperation, their bodies contorted in anguish. The contrast between light and shadow, as well as the use of powerful diagonal lines, heightens the sense of chaos and movement. Géricault's meticulous attention to detail, including his study of corpses and interviews with survivors, brings an almost unbearable realism to the scene. *The Raft of the Medusa* is not just a stunning example of Romanticism; it is also a powerful political statement about the corruption and incompetence of the French government at the time. Géricault's willingness to confront such a controversial subject, combined with the emotional intensity of the painting, has made it one of the Louvre's most gripping masterpieces.

Equally significant in the Louvre's collection is the *Venus de Milo*, an ancient Greek statue of Aphrodite, the goddess of love and beauty. Discovered on the Greek island of Melos in 1820, this marble sculpture dates back to around 100 BCE and is attributed to the sculptor Alexandros of Antioch. Standing over six feet tall, the *Venus de Milo* is admired for its graceful form and the idealized beauty of the goddess.

Despite missing her arms, the statue exudes a sense of elegance and poise. The drapery that partially covers her lower body is masterfully carved, giving the impression of softness and movement, contrasting with the smooth, polished surface of her skin. The *Venus de Milo* represents the Hellenistic ideals of beauty and physical perfection, and its allure lies in the way it captures the divine and the human in one harmonious form. The statue's discovery in the 19th century stirred considerable excitement, and it was quickly acquired by the French government and placed in the Louvre. Over time, the *Venus de Milo* has become one of the most famous sculptures in the world, embodying the timeless appeal of classical art.

Another iconic piece in the Louvre is the *Winged Victory of Samothrace*, an ancient Greek sculpture that dates back to the 2nd century BCE. Also known as the *Nike of Samothrace*, this stunning statue depicts the goddess Nike, the personification of victory, as she alights on the prow of a ship. The *Winged Victory* is celebrated for its dynamic sense of movement and the sheer power it conveys. The goddess's wings are outstretched, and her drapery seems to be blown back by the wind, giving the impression that she is descending from the heavens. The intricacies of the folds in the fabric and the sense of motion in the statue's form are remarkable, creating a breathtaking example of Hellenistic sculpture. Discovered on the island of Samothrace in 1863, the statue was originally part of a larger monument commemorating a naval victory. Although the figure is missing its head and arms, the *Winged Victory of Samothrace* retains an extraordinary presence and is often considered one of the most sublime representations of the human form in art. Positioned at the top of the Daru staircase in the Louvre, it greets visitors as they ascend, its commanding posture symbolizing triumph and strength.

Another major highlight of the Louvre's collection is *Liberty Leading the People* by Eugène Delacroix, painted in 1830. This powerful work captures a moment from the July Revolution of 1830, when the people of Paris rose up against the repressive rule of King Charles X. At the center of the composition is Liberty herself, personified as a robust, allegorical figure holding the French tricolor flag in one hand and a musket in the other. She is bare-breasted, symbolizing both her maternal role as the protector of the people and the idea of freedom breaking free from the constraints of tyranny. Around her are revolutionaries from different classes of society: a young boy wielding pistols, a working-class man in a vest and cap, and a bourgeois intellectual. The smoke-filled battlefield is littered with the bodies of the fallen, but the figures following Liberty surge forward with determination and hope. Delacroix's bold use of color, particularly the red, white, and blue of the French flag, along with the dramatic lighting and chaotic energy of the scene, make *Liberty Leading the People* one of the most stirring political paintings in art history. It encapsulates the spirit of revolution and the universal struggle for freedom and equality, resonating far beyond its specific historical context.

One cannot discuss the Louvre's masterpieces without mentioning *The Coronation of Napoleon*, painted by Jacques-Louis David between 1805 and 1807. This monumental painting, which measures over 20 feet in width, depicts the coronation ceremony of Napoleon Bonaparte, held in Notre-Dame Cathedral in 1804. David, the official court painter to Napoleon, was commissioned to commemorate the event, and his depiction is both grandiose and meticulously detailed. The painting captures the moment when Napoleon crowns his wife, Joséphine, in front of a gathered audience of dignitaries, clergy, and military officials. Napoleon, standing tall and confident, places the crown on Joséphine's head, asserting his dominance not only as a military leader but as the self-proclaimed emperor of France. The composition is filled with symbolic elements, from the golden laurel wreath atop Napoleon's head (a nod to Roman emperors) to the presence of Pope Pius VII, who watches the scene passively, reflecting the complex relationship between the church and the new emperor. David's mastery of neoclassical style, with its emphasis on clarity, precision, and grandeur, is on full display in this work. *The Coronation of Napoleon* not only glorifies the rise of Napoleon but also serves as a testament to the artist's ability to capture the political ambitions of his time.

Sculpture is also well represented at the Louvre, and one of the most famous examples is Michelangelo's *Dying Slave*. Created between 1513 and 1516 as part of a larger, unfinished project for the tomb of Pope Julius II, the *Dying Slave* is one of two figures (along with the *Rebellious Slave*) that Michelangelo sculpted to symbolize the struggle between life and death. The *Dying Slave* is a hauntingly beautiful figure, caught in a moment of extreme vulnerability. His body, bound in chains, leans backward in a graceful yet agonized pose, as though he is succumbing to the inevitable pull of death. Michelangelo's ability to convey the tension between strength and helplessness is unparalleled, and the intricate detailing of the muscles and veins in the figure's body gives the sculpture a remarkable sense of realism. The *Dying Slave* exemplifies the artist's mastery of anatomy and his deep understanding of the human condition, making it one of the Louvre's most moving masterpieces.

These are just a few of the masterpieces that define the Louvre's collection. The museum is home to countless other works of art that span the entirety of human civilization, from ancient Mesopotamian artifacts like the *Code of Hammurabi* to Renaissance masterpieces such as *The Madonna of the Rocks* by Leonardo da Vinci, and even modern works like *Le Bain Turc* by Jean-Auguste-Dominique Ingres. Each work in the Louvre's vast collection tells a story, and together, they offer an unparalleled journey through the history of art. Visitors to the museum are not merely spectators; they are participants in a centuries-long dialogue between artists, patrons, and viewers, all seeking to understand the world and their place within it through the lens of artistic expression. The masterpieces housed in the Louvre are timeless, offering inspiration, reflection, and insight to all who behold them.

Chapter 5: The Mona Lisa's Journey to Fame

The journey of Leonardo da Vinci's *Mona Lisa* from a relatively obscure portrait to the most famous painting in the world is a fascinating story filled with historical intrigue, art-world scandals, technical brilliance, and shifting cultural dynamics. Today, the *Mona Lisa* stands as not only the centerpiece of the Louvre Museum but also a symbol of artistic genius, cultural history, and the enigmatic power of art. Her fame is unparalleled, drawing millions of visitors each year who come to witness her captivating smile and mysterious gaze. Yet, her rise to global stardom was not instantaneous. The story of how the *Mona Lisa* achieved this iconic status involves centuries of rediscovery, dramatic theft, innovative media coverage, and the enduring fascination with her subject matter.

The painting was created by Leonardo da Vinci between 1503 and 1506, during the height of the Italian Renaissance. Commissioned by a wealthy Florentine merchant, Francesco del Giocondo, it was intended to be a portrait of his wife, Lisa Gherardini. The portrait itself was not particularly unique for its time; Renaissance artists frequently painted portraits of wealthy individuals to commemorate their status and wealth. However, da Vinci's technique in painting the *Mona Lisa* set it apart. Da Vinci employed a method known as *sfumato*, a technique that uses subtle gradations of light and shadow to create a lifelike softness in the skin and features, without the harsh lines that other artists of the time used. The smooth transitions and blending of tones give the *Mona Lisa* her famously serene and mysterious expression, as if she is both smiling and not smiling at the same time. Her eyes seem to follow the viewer around the room, adding to the painting's eerie sense of realism. Da Vinci's mastery of anatomical precision, combined with this delicate handling of light and shadow, contributed to the *Mona Lisa*'s uniqueness as a piece of art.

Despite this technical brilliance, the *Mona Lisa* was not particularly famous during da Vinci's lifetime. After completing the portrait, da Vinci never delivered it to the original commissioner and instead kept the painting with him when he moved to France to work for King Francis I in 1516. Upon his death in 1519, the painting was acquired by the French royal collection and eventually made its way to the Louvre in the late 18th century. For centuries, the *Mona Lisa* remained relatively unknown, admired by art connoisseurs but not celebrated as a cultural phenomenon. It was simply one of many Renaissance paintings housed in the Louvre's massive collection.

It wasn't until the 19th century that the *Mona Lisa* began to gain attention. The rise of Romanticism in European art and culture brought with it a renewed interest in Leonardo da Vinci, who was seen as a genius whose work embodied the ideals of the Renaissance. Writers, poets, and art critics began to praise the *Mona Lisa* for her ethereal beauty and enigmatic expression, and she slowly started to gain recognition as one of Leonardo's finest works. However, the painting's fame was still largely limited to Europe and the art world's elite, as the general public had little exposure to the work, which remained tucked away in the Louvre's collection.

The event that truly launched the *Mona Lisa* into the global spotlight occurred in 1911, when the painting was stolen from the Louvre. The thief, an Italian named Vincenzo Peruggia, was a former museum employee who believed that the painting rightfully belonged in Italy, as it had been painted by an Italian master. Peruggia and his accomplices snuck into the museum during daylight, removed the painting from its frame, and hid it under a workman's smock before fleeing the building. When the theft was discovered the next day, it sent shockwaves throughout the art world and beyond. The *Mona Lisa*'s disappearance became a major international news story, captivating the public and sparking widespread outrage and fascination. Newspapers across the world ran stories about the missing masterpiece, and for two years, the whereabouts of the painting remained a mystery. During this time, replicas of the *Mona Lisa* were created and circulated in the press, further cementing her image in the public imagination. The theft turned the *Mona Lisa* from a relatively well-known painting into a global sensation.

In 1913, the painting was finally recovered when Peruggia attempted to sell it to an art dealer in Florence. The dealer, suspicious of the painting's provenance, contacted the authorities, and Peruggia was arrested. The *Mona Lisa* was returned to the Louvre, where it was greeted with widespread celebration. The dramatic recovery of the painting only added to its mystique, and it solidified its place as one of the most famous works of art in the world. The *Mona Lisa*'s theft and recovery became a legend, transforming her from a beautiful but relatively obscure painting into a symbol of national pride and artistic greatness.

By the mid-20th century, the *Mona Lisa* had fully entered the realm of cultural iconography. The invention of photography and the growing accessibility of travel meant that more people than ever before could see images of the painting or visit the Louvre in person. Art historians and critics continued to analyze and reinterpret the *Mona Lisa*'s enigmatic expression, debating whether her smile represented happiness, sadness, or even something more profound, such as divine wisdom or eternal knowledge. This sense of mystery contributed to the growing fascination with the painting. The *Mona Lisa*'s fame also spread due to its frequent reproductions in art books, posters, and postcards, turning her image into a familiar sight even for those who had never visited the Louvre. The painting's iconic status was further cemented by its inclusion in pop culture, with artists like Salvador Dalí and Marcel Duchamp incorporating the *Mona Lisa* into their work as a commentary on art and fame. Duchamp's *L.H.O.O.Q.*, in which he added a mustache and goatee to a reproduction of the *Mona Lisa*, was a playful yet provocative gesture that highlighted the painting's transformation into a cultural artifact.

One of the key moments in the *Mona Lisa*'s journey to worldwide fame came in 1963 when the painting was loaned to the United States for a special exhibition. The French government, under the leadership of President Charles de Gaulle, agreed to send the painting on a highly publicized tour of Washington, D.C., and New York City as a gesture of goodwill between France and the United States. The tour was an unprecedented event; never before had a painting been transported with such care and security. The *Mona Lisa* was displayed under bulletproof glass, with armed guards constantly monitoring it. In Washington, it was exhibited at the National Gallery of Art, where it was viewed by over half a million people, including President John F. Kennedy and First Lady Jacqueline Kennedy. The *Mona Lisa* was then sent to the Metropolitan Museum of Art in New York, where similar crowds gathered to see the painting. The *Mona Lisa*'s tour of the United States turned her into a media sensation, with television and newspaper coverage bringing her image into millions of American homes. The tour made the painting a symbol not just of French art, but of Western culture as a whole. Her image became synonymous with high art and sophistication, and the *Mona Lisa* solidified her status as the most famous painting in the world.

In the decades that followed, the *Mona Lisa*'s fame only continued to grow. The painting became the subject of academic research, with scholars studying everything from Leonardo's painting techniques to the identity of the woman portrayed in the work. Some have speculated that the *Mona Lisa* might be a self-portrait of Leonardo in disguise, while others suggest that her enigmatic smile reflects complex psychological theories about emotion and perception. The *Mona Lisa*'s allure lies not only in her technical mastery but also in the many unanswered questions that surround her. This sense of mystery has kept viewers fascinated, as each generation brings new interpretations and theories about what the painting represents.

The painting's fame also attracted a number of dramatic incidents. In 1956, a man threw acid at the lower half of the painting, damaging part of the work. Fortunately, the damage was minor and was later restored. In another attack, a Bolivian visitor threw a rock at the painting, chipping the paint near the left elbow. As a result of these incidents, the Louvre took even greater precautions to protect the *Mona Lisa*, placing it behind bulletproof glass and employing increased security measures. These attacks, while unfortunate, only added to the painting's mythos, reinforcing the idea that the *Mona Lisa* was an artwork of immense value and significance, worth protecting at all costs.

The 21st century has seen the *Mona Lisa* continue to evolve as both an artwork and a cultural symbol. The rise of the internet and social media has introduced the painting to a new generation of viewers, many of whom may never see it in person but are nonetheless familiar with its image. The *Mona Lisa*'s image has been meme-ified, reinterpreted, and reimagined in countless ways, further embedding it into the global cultural consciousness. The painting's ubiquity, combined with its historical significance and artistic brilliance, has made it a symbol of art's enduring power to captivate and inspire.

In recent years, the *Mona Lisa* has faced the challenges of being the most popular attraction in the Louvre. The museum now attracts over 10 million visitors per year, many of whom come specifically to see the painting. This influx of visitors has led to long lines and crowded viewing conditions, as the painting is relatively small compared to the massive galleries that house it. However, for most visitors, the chance to stand before the *Mona Lisa*—even if only for a brief moment—is an unforgettable experience.

Ultimately, the *Mona Lisa*'s journey to fame is a testament to the power of art to transcend time, space, and cultural boundaries. From a modest portrait in Renaissance Italy to a global icon, the painting has evolved into a symbol of artistic excellence, human curiosity, and the mysteries that lie within the human soul. Whether admired for her beauty, her history, or her elusive smile, the *Mona Lisa* continues to captivate, reminding us of the profound impact that a single work of art can have on the world.

Chapter 6: The Ancient Egyptian Collection at the Louvre

The Ancient Egyptian collection at the Louvre Museum is one of the most extensive and impressive collections of Egyptian artifacts in the world, rivaled only by a few institutions such as the British Museum and the Egyptian Museum in Cairo. This extraordinary collection spans more than 4,000 years of ancient Egyptian history, encompassing objects from the Predynastic Period (around 4000 BCE) through the Greco-Roman period in Egypt, up to the 4th century CE. The collection contains over 50,000 objects, with around 6,000 of these items on permanent display in the museum. From monumental sculptures and intricate jewelry to religious artifacts, tools, and texts, the collection provides a comprehensive look into the daily life, religious beliefs, artistic achievements, and funerary practices of ancient Egypt. The collection is not only an invaluable resource for scholars and archaeologists but also a favorite among visitors of all ages, offering a fascinating glimpse into one of the world's most advanced and mysterious ancient civilizations.

The Louvre's journey toward building its prestigious Egyptian collection began during the Napoleonic campaigns in Egypt between 1798 and 1801. Napoleon Bonaparte, fascinated by ancient Egypt, led a military expedition to the region that included a team of scholars, scientists, and archaeologists. This endeavor marked the birth of modern Egyptology and resulted in the famous publication of *Description de l'Égypte*, a monumental work that cataloged the ancient monuments, artifacts, and customs of Egypt as observed by Napoleon's team. Although the campaign itself did not directly bring many Egyptian artifacts to the Louvre, it sparked widespread interest in Egyptian history and culture, fueling a wave of archaeological expeditions throughout the 19th century. France became one of the foremost centers of Egyptological study, and over time, the Louvre began to amass its collection through donations, acquisitions, and archaeological discoveries.

A key figure in the formation of the Louvre's Egyptian department was Jean-François Champollion, the brilliant French scholar who famously deciphered the Rosetta Stone in 1822, unlocking the secrets of Egyptian hieroglyphs for the first time in centuries. Champollion's work in understanding the Egyptian language revolutionized the study of ancient Egypt and contributed to the Louvre's interest in building a comprehensive Egyptian collection. He was instrumental in acquiring many of the artifacts that now form the core of the Louvre's holdings, helping to establish the museum's Egyptian Antiquities Department in 1827. Champollion himself visited Egypt in the late 1820s, where he selected numerous objects that were transported back to France, including statues, stelae, sarcophagi, and other items of artistic and historical significance.

One of the crowning jewels of the Louvre's Egyptian collection is the *Seated Scribe*, an extraordinary statue that dates back to the Old Kingdom period (around 2600-2350 BCE). This limestone statue depicts a scribe sitting cross-legged, with a papyrus scroll resting on his lap. The figure's lifelike features, including his slightly alert expression, painted eyes, and realistic body shape, make it one of the most striking and well-preserved statues from ancient Egypt. The *Seated Scribe* is notable not only for its artistic quality but also for its depiction of a social class that played a critical role in Egyptian society. Scribes were highly respected in ancient Egypt, as they were responsible for recording important religious, administrative, and economic documents. The statue's vibrant portrayal of a scribe at work serves as a window into the daily life of the literate elite in ancient Egypt, and it is widely regarded as one of the most iconic pieces in the Louvre's collection.

The Louvre's collection also features a number of large-scale sculptures, including the colossal statue of the pharaoh *Ramses II*, one of ancient Egypt's most powerful and renowned rulers. Ramses II, who reigned during the 19th Dynasty (1279–1213 BCE), is often considered one of the greatest pharaohs of the New Kingdom period, known for his military exploits, monumental building projects, and the peace treaty he signed with the Hittites after the famous Battle of Kadesh. The statue of Ramses II in the Louvre depicts the pharaoh seated on a throne, wearing the nemes headdress and the royal false beard, symbols of his divine kingship. This sculpture, made of red granite, is an imposing representation of Ramses' power and authority, and its finely carved details highlight the artistry and skill of ancient Egyptian sculptors. Such monumental sculptures were often placed in temples or other sacred spaces to reinforce the divine status of the pharaoh and to ensure his eternal presence in the spiritual realm.

Among the most significant artifacts in the Louvre's Egyptian collection is the *Great Sphinx of Tanis*, a massive stone sculpture that is one of the largest sphinxes outside of Egypt. Carved from a single block of red granite, the sphinx dates back to the 12th Dynasty (around 1900 BCE) and was found in the ruins of the Temple of Amun at Tanis, an ancient city in the Nile Delta. Like the more famous Great Sphinx of Giza, the *Great Sphinx of Tanis* combines the body of a lion with the head of a pharaoh, symbolizing the pharaoh's strength and wisdom. This particular sphinx is thought to represent Pharaoh Amenemhat II, although later pharaohs may have re-carved or reused the statue for their own purposes. The sphinx's size and grandeur make it one of the most impressive pieces in the Louvre's collection, and it stands as a testament to the ancient Egyptians' mastery of large-scale stone sculpture and their reverence for the symbolism of the sphinx in representing royal power and divine protection.

Funerary artifacts, including sarcophagi, canopic jars, and ushabti figurines, form an essential part of the Louvre's Egyptian collection, offering insights into ancient Egyptian beliefs about death and the afterlife. One of the most striking pieces in this category is the *Sarcophagus of Ramesses III*, a massive stone sarcophagus that once housed the body of the last great pharaoh of the New Kingdom. Ramesses III reigned from 1186 to 1155 BCE and is known for defending Egypt from invasions by the Sea Peoples and for maintaining a relatively stable and prosperous rule. His sarcophagus, intricately carved with hieroglyphs and images of protective deities, reflects the Egyptians' belief in the afterlife and the importance of ensuring the deceased's safe passage to the realm of the gods. The sarcophagus is a stunning example of ancient Egyptian funerary art, with detailed scenes of the pharaoh's journey through the underworld and his eventual rebirth as an immortal being. The imagery on the sarcophagus highlights the central role that religion and the concept of eternal life played in Egyptian society, as well as the artistic skill involved in creating these elaborate burial items.

The Louvre's collection also includes numerous objects related to daily life in ancient Egypt, such as pottery, tools, jewelry, and household items. These artifacts offer a glimpse into the everyday experiences of ancient Egyptians, from farmers and craftsmen to members of the elite. For example, the museum houses an impressive collection of amulets and jewelry, many of which were believed to possess protective or magical properties. Amulets shaped like the *ankh* (the symbol of life), the *scarab* beetle (a symbol of rebirth), and the *Eye of Horus* (a symbol of protection) were commonly worn by Egyptians or placed in tombs to ensure the safety and well-being of the deceased in the afterlife. The craftsmanship of these pieces, made from materials such as gold, silver, faience, and semi-precious stones, showcases the high level of skill achieved by ancient Egyptian artisans.

Papyrus scrolls and inscriptions from the Louvre's collection provide invaluable information about the religious, administrative, and literary life of ancient Egypt. One of the most important texts in the museum is a version of the *Book of the Dead*, an ancient funerary text that served as a guide for the deceased on their journey through the underworld. The *Book of the Dead* contains a series of spells, prayers, and incantations meant to protect the soul and help it overcome obstacles in the afterlife. These texts, often illustrated with detailed vignettes, were placed in tombs to assist the deceased in achieving eternal life. The Louvre's collection includes several beautifully preserved papyri that depict scenes from the afterlife, including the famous "weighing of the heart" ceremony, in which the deceased's heart is weighed against the feather of truth to determine whether they are worthy of entering the afterlife.

One of the most significant architectural artifacts in the Louvre's Egyptian collection is the *Chapel of Akhethotep*, an entire tomb chapel that was transported from its original location in Saqqara, the ancient burial ground near Memphis. Akhethotep was a high-ranking official during the Fifth Dynasty (around 2400 BCE), and his tomb chapel is adorned with intricately carved reliefs depicting scenes from his life and the various rituals associated with the afterlife. The chapel's reliefs show Akhethotep engaged in activities such as hunting, fishing, and making offerings to the gods, providing a detailed picture of the religious and social practices of the Egyptian elite during this period. The chapel's relocation to the Louvre is a remarkable example of the lengths taken to preserve and display ancient Egyptian architecture, allowing visitors to experience a piece of ancient Egypt in the heart of Paris.

Another major highlight of the Egyptian collection is the array of statues representing gods and goddesses, reflecting the central role of religion in ancient Egyptian life. Statues of deities such as *Osiris*, the god of the afterlife, *Isis*, the mother goddess, and *Horus*, the falcon-headed god of the sky, are all represented in the Louvre's collection. These statues, often made from bronze, stone, or wood, were used in temples and shrines as part of religious rituals and were believed to house the divine spirit of the god or goddess they represented. The Louvre's statues of Egyptian deities range from small figurines to larger-than-life sculptures, demonstrating the importance of religious iconography in both personal and state-sponsored worship.

The collection's significance goes beyond just art and artifacts; it represents centuries of cultural exchange, the intersection of history, religion, and politics, and the enduring human fascination with the mysteries of life, death, and the divine.

Chapter 7: Greek and Roman Art Treasures

The Louvre Museum houses one of the most extensive and remarkable collections of Greek and Roman art treasures in the world. Spanning from the archaic period of ancient Greece to the fall of the Roman Empire, this collection represents over a millennium of artistic, cultural, and intellectual achievements that have had a profound influence on Western civilization. These treasures offer an unparalleled window into the art, politics, philosophy, and religious beliefs of the ancient Mediterranean world, reflecting the beauty, power, and complexity of Greek and Roman societies. The Louvre's Greek and Roman galleries are home to masterpieces of sculpture, pottery, jewelry, and architectural fragments, each telling a story of the civilizations that produced them and the enduring legacy they left behind.

The origins of the Louvre's collection of Greek and Roman antiquities date back to the 17th century when France began acquiring classical artifacts during the reign of Louis XIV. However, the collection truly began to expand during the Napoleonic era, when French military campaigns across Europe brought a wealth of ancient treasures to the Louvre. Napoleon's conquests in Italy, Greece, and Egypt led to the seizure of numerous classical works, many of which were brought back to Paris and added to the Louvre's growing collection. Over time, as archaeological excavations uncovered more ancient sites and private collectors donated their acquisitions to the museum, the Louvre's Greek and Roman collection became one of the largest and most important in the world. Today, the collection is housed in the museum's Denon and Sully wings, where it draws millions of visitors each year who come to admire its rich and varied offerings.

One of the most famous and iconic pieces in the Louvre's Greek collection is the *Venus de Milo*, an ancient Greek statue that has become a symbol of classical beauty and grace. Discovered on the island of Melos (also known as Milos) in 1820, the statue is believed to have been created between 130 and 100 BCE, during the Hellenistic period. The *Venus de Milo* is a depiction of Aphrodite, the Greek goddess of love and beauty, and stands over six feet tall, with flowing drapery around her lower body and an exposed torso. Although the statue's arms have been lost, her serene expression and balanced, elegant proportions have captivated viewers for centuries. The statue is renowned for its harmonious blend of idealized beauty and naturalism, characteristics that were highly valued in Hellenistic art. The *Venus de Milo's* pose, with its subtle twist of the torso and gentle tilt of the head, exemplifies the classical Greek aesthetic, which sought to portray the human body in a state of dynamic equilibrium. The statue's discovery and subsequent display at the Louvre have made it one of the most celebrated sculptures in the world, and it remains one of the museum's most visited works of art.

Another masterpiece of ancient Greek art in the Louvre is the *Winged Victory of Samothrace*, a monumental statue that stands at the top of the museum's grand staircase. The *Winged Victory* (also known as the *Nike of Samothrace*) is a Hellenistic sculpture created around 190 BCE to commemorate a naval victory. The statue represents Nike, the Greek goddess of victory, with her wings outstretched and her drapery billowing in the wind as she alights on the prow of a ship. Although the statue's head and arms are missing, the remaining figure conveys a powerful sense of movement and energy, as if the goddess is about to take flight. The skillful rendering of the folds of her garments, which cling to her body and flutter in the air, demonstrates the mastery of Hellenistic sculptors in creating a sense of dynamism and realism. The *Winged Victory of Samothrace* was discovered in the 19th century on the island of Samothrace in the northern Aegean Sea, where it had been part of a sanctuary dedicated to the gods of the sea. Its dramatic display at the Louvre, perched on a marble staircase with light streaming in from above, enhances its sense of grandeur and awe, making it one of the museum's most visually striking works.

The Louvre's collection of Greek pottery is equally impressive, offering a glimpse into the daily life, mythology, and artistic practices of ancient Greece. Greek pottery, particularly from the Archaic and Classical periods, is known for its distinctive shapes and intricate painted designs, often depicting scenes from mythology, athletics, and everyday life. One of the most famous examples in the Louvre's collection is the *François Vase*, a large black-figure krater created around 570 BCE by the potter Ergotimos and the painter Kleitias. The *François Vase* is decorated with multiple registers of detailed narrative scenes, including depictions of the wedding of Peleus and Thetis, the Calydonian Boar Hunt, and the funeral games for Patroclus, all drawn from Greek mythology. The vase is a masterpiece of the black-figure technique, in which figures and scenes are painted in black on a red clay background, with fine incised details added to enhance the figures' features and clothing. The precision and complexity of the scenes on the *François Vase* showcase the high level of artistry achieved by Greek potters and painters, as well as the importance of mythological storytelling in Greek culture.

The Louvre's Roman collection is equally rich and diverse, reflecting the grandeur and complexity of the Roman Empire at its height. Roman art was deeply influenced by Greek precedents, but it also developed its own distinctive style, characterized by a greater emphasis on realism and individuality in portraiture, as well as a fascination with monumental architecture and public sculpture. One of the most famous Roman sculptures in the Louvre is the *Bust of Emperor Augustus*, a marble portrait that captures the first Roman emperor in a serene and idealized pose. Augustus, who ruled from 27 BCE to 14 CE, was a master of political propaganda, and his portraits were carefully crafted to present him as a godlike figure, embodying the ideals of peace, stability, and divine favor. The *Bust of Augustus* exemplifies this idealized representation, with its smooth, youthful features and calm expression conveying a sense of authority and dignity. Roman portraiture was known for its ability to combine realism with idealization, creating images of rulers and elites that were both recognizable and aspirational.

Another highlight of the Louvre's Roman collection is the *Sarcophagus of the Spouses*, an Etruscan funerary monument that dates back to the 6th century BCE. The sarcophagus, made of terracotta, depicts a reclining couple lying side by side on a couch, as if attending a banquet. The figures are shown in a tender, intimate pose, with the man's arm draped affectionately around the woman's shoulders. The *Sarcophagus of the Spouses* is an exceptional example of Etruscan funerary art, which often emphasized the idea of the afterlife as a continuation of the joys of life, particularly the pleasures of dining and socializing. The sarcophagus also reflects the relatively high status of women in Etruscan society, where women were often depicted as active participants in social and religious life, in contrast to the more restricted roles they played in Greek and Roman society. The Louvre's collection of Etruscan art, which includes bronzes, pottery, and jewelry, offers valuable insights into this influential but often overlooked civilization, which played a key role in shaping early Roman culture.

The Louvre is also home to an impressive collection of Roman mosaics, many of which were discovered in ancient Roman villas and public buildings. Roman mosaics, created from small pieces of colored stone, glass, or ceramic, were used to decorate floors, walls, and ceilings, and they often depicted elaborate scenes from mythology, history, or daily life. One of the most famous mosaics in the Louvre's collection is the *Mosaic of the Battle of Issus*, which depicts the dramatic encounter between Alexander the Great and the Persian king Darius III during the Battle of Issus in 333 BCE. The mosaic, made from thousands of tiny tesserae, captures the intensity of the battle, with detailed depictions of horses, soldiers, and weapons in the midst of combat. The *Mosaic of the Battle of Issus* is a stunning example of Roman craftsmanship and artistic skill, and it reflects the Roman fascination with historical and mythological themes.

The Louvre's collection of architectural fragments from ancient Greece and Rome is another significant aspect of its Greek and Roman art treasures. These fragments, which include columns, capitals, friezes, and other decorative elements, provide a glimpse into the monumental scale and grandeur of ancient temples, palaces, and public buildings. One of the most famous architectural pieces in the Louvre is the *Parthenon Frieze*, a series of sculpted panels that once adorned the exterior of the Parthenon, the great temple to Athena in Athens. The frieze depicts a procession of figures, including gods, goddesses, and mortals, participating in a religious festival in honor of Athena. The figures are rendered with exquisite detail and grace, and the frieze is a testament to the skill and creativity of the Athenian sculptors who worked on the Parthenon under the direction of the great architect Phidias. The *Parthenon Frieze* is a reminder of the central role that religion, civic pride, and artistic achievement played in the life of ancient Athens, and it remains one of the most important surviving examples of classical Greek art.

The Louvre's Greek and Roman collection also includes a wide variety of smaller artifacts, such as jewelry, coins, and household items, which offer insights into the everyday life of the ancient Mediterranean world. Greek and Roman jewelry, often made from gold, silver, and precious stones, was not only a symbol of wealth and status but also served religious and protective purposes. Many pieces of jewelry in the Louvre's collection, such as necklaces, bracelets, and rings, feature intricate designs and symbols, including depictions of gods and goddesses, animals, and mythological creatures. Roman coins, another important part of the collection, provide valuable information about the political and economic history of the Roman Empire. Coins were often minted to commemorate important events, such as military victories or the ascension of a new emperor, and they feature portraits of emperors and empresses, as well as symbols of power and divinity.

In conclusion, the Greek and Roman art treasures at the Louvre offer an unparalleled exploration of two of the most influential civilizations in Western history. From monumental sculptures like the *Venus de Milo* and the *Winged Victory of Samothrace* to intricate pottery, jewelry, and mosaics, the collection captures the artistic brilliance and cultural richness of ancient Greece and Rome. The artifacts in the Louvre's collection provide not only aesthetic beauty but also a deep understanding of the social, political, and religious values that shaped these civilizations. The Greek and Roman galleries at the Louvre remain a testament to the enduring legacy of classical art and its continued ability to inspire awe and admiration in viewers from around the world.

Chapter 8: Discovering the Islamic Art Exhibit

The Louvre's Islamic Art Exhibit is a treasure trove of cultural and artistic wonders that celebrates over a millennium of Islamic civilization, spanning from the 7th century to the 19th century. This expansive collection includes artifacts from across the Islamic world, covering a vast geographical region that stretches from Spain and North Africa to the Middle East, Iran, India, and Central Asia. It encompasses a wide variety of mediums—ceramics, metalwork, textiles, glass, ivory, wood, and manuscripts—each reflecting the unique aesthetic, religious, and social values of the Islamic world. The Louvre's Islamic Art collection is one of the most comprehensive in the world, and its exhibition is housed in the striking and modern Islamic Art Department, a relatively new addition to the museum, inaugurated in 2012. The exhibit not only showcases the extraordinary beauty of Islamic art but also serves as a bridge between cultures, fostering greater understanding and appreciation of the rich heritage of the Muslim world.

Islamic art is notable for its intricate patterns, vibrant colors, and emphasis on geometric and abstract forms. Unlike Western art traditions that often focused on the depiction of the human form, Islamic art developed its own distinctive visual language that was heavily influenced by religious beliefs. In particular, the prohibition against figural representation in religious contexts—derived from certain interpretations of Islamic teachings—led to a focus on non-figurative art forms, such as calligraphy, arabesque patterns, and geometric designs. These forms were used to decorate religious buildings, manuscripts, ceramics, and textiles, creating a visual language that expressed the divine through abstraction and symbolism. Calligraphy, in particular, became one of the highest forms of artistic expression in the Islamic world, as the written word, especially verses from the Quran, was considered a direct manifestation of God's will. The Islamic Art Exhibit at the Louvre showcases numerous examples of calligraphy, including manuscripts, inscriptions, and illuminated texts, all of which demonstrate the skill and reverence with which Muslim artists approached the written word.

One of the highlights of the Louvre's Islamic Art collection is its display of illuminated manuscripts, many of which are copies of the Quran, Islam's holy book. These manuscripts are not only religious texts but also stunning works of art, adorned with intricate patterns, gold leaf, and vivid colors. The calligraphy used to write the Quran, most often in the elegant scripts of Kufic, Naskh, and Thuluth, is meticulously crafted, with each letter and word given great attention to detail. The margins of the pages are often decorated with floral motifs, arabesques, and geometric designs, which serve both to beautify the text and to reflect the infinite nature of God's creation. The manuscripts in the Louvre's collection come from various parts of the Islamic world, reflecting the diversity of styles and techniques developed in different regions. For example, Persian illuminated manuscripts often feature intricate miniature paintings that accompany the text, while Ottoman and Mamluk manuscripts may emphasize bold, large-scale calligraphy with lavish gold embellishments. These manuscripts are a testament to the central role that the Quran and the written word played in Islamic culture, serving as both a spiritual guide and a source of artistic inspiration.

The Louvre's collection of ceramics from the Islamic world is another highlight of the Islamic Art Exhibit, offering a glimpse into the artistic and technical innovations that flourished in pottery production throughout the Islamic empire. Islamic potters were renowned for their ability to create highly decorative and durable ceramics, and their work had a profound influence on the development of pottery in Europe and Asia. One of the most famous techniques developed by Islamic potters is lustreware, a type of pottery that achieves a shimmering, metallic glaze through the use of a complex firing process. Lustreware was particularly popular in the Abbasid caliphate during the 9th and 10th centuries and later spread to Spain and Persia. The Louvre's collection includes several stunning examples of lustreware, featuring intricate designs in gold, silver, and copper tones. Many of these pieces are decorated with geometric patterns, floral motifs, or calligraphic inscriptions, reflecting the Islamic emphasis on abstraction and the beauty of form.

Another significant type of Islamic ceramics represented in the Louvre is Iznik pottery, produced in the Ottoman Empire, especially during the 16th and 17th centuries. Iznik pottery is known for its bold colors, particularly the use of cobalt blue, turquoise, and red, as well as its intricate floral and vegetal designs. The Iznik style was heavily influenced by earlier Persian pottery and Chinese porcelain, but it developed its own unique aesthetic under the patronage of the Ottoman court. Many of the plates, tiles, and vessels from Iznik found in the Louvre's collection feature the iconic tulip and carnation motifs, which were symbols of the Ottoman Empire. These vibrant and detailed ceramics were used to decorate the interiors of mosques, palaces, and other important buildings, reflecting the Ottoman love of luxury and refinement. In addition to Iznik pottery, the Louvre's Islamic Art Exhibit includes ceramics from other important centers of production, such as Kashan in Persia, where potters developed advanced techniques in underglaze painting and overglaze decoration.

Metalwork is another area where Islamic artists excelled, and the Louvre's Islamic Art Exhibit features an impressive array of metal objects, including lamps, bowls, ewers, and weapons. Islamic metalworkers were masters of techniques such as inlaying, engraving, and gilding, often using precious metals like gold and silver to create intricate designs on bronze or brass objects. Many of these metal objects were used in religious or ceremonial contexts, such as mosque lamps, which were often inscribed with verses from the Quran or the names of patrons who donated them. The Louvre's collection includes several magnificent mosque lamps, some of which are decorated with elaborate enamel work and gold inscriptions. One of the most famous examples of Islamic metalwork in the Louvre is the *Baptistère de Saint Louis*, a large brass basin inlaid with silver and gold, created in the Mamluk period in Egypt or Syria around the 14th century. The basin is decorated with scenes of hunting, feasting, and battle, as well as intricate arabesque patterns and calligraphic inscriptions. Despite its Islamic origins, the basin was later used in France for the baptism of French kings, including Louis XIII, giving it a fascinating cross-cultural history.

Glassmaking also reached new heights in the Islamic world, and the Louvre's Islamic Art Exhibit showcases some of the finest examples of Islamic glasswork, including blown glass vessels, stained glass windows, and enamelled glass lamps. Islamic glassmakers were known for their technical expertise and innovation, producing a wide variety of shapes and designs that were highly prized throughout the medieval world. Many of the glass objects in the Louvre's collection, such as perfume bottles, drinking vessels, and decorative lamps, are adorned with intricate patterns and vivid colors, often achieved through the use of enamel and gilding. One of the most striking examples of Islamic glass in the Louvre's collection is a 14th-century enamelled glass lamp from Egypt, which features a beautifully painted design of flowers and Arabic calligraphy. This type of lamp would have been used to illuminate a mosque or religious school, adding both light and beauty to the sacred space.

Textiles also hold a prominent place in the Louvre's Islamic Art Exhibit, reflecting the importance of fabric in the Islamic world, both as a functional commodity and as a form of artistic expression. The Islamic world was renowned for its production of luxurious textiles, including silk, wool, and cotton, often adorned with intricate embroidery, brocade, and weaving techniques. The Louvre's collection includes textiles from various regions, such as Persian carpets, Ottoman kaftans, and Andalusian silk panels. These textiles were not only used for clothing and furnishings but also served as diplomatic gifts and trade items, spreading Islamic artistic influences across Europe and Asia. One of the most remarkable textiles in the Louvre's collection is a Mamluk carpet from the 15th century, which features a complex geometric design in vibrant reds, blues, and golds. The intricate patterns of Islamic textiles, often based on geometric and floral motifs, reflect the same principles of abstraction and symmetry that are found in other forms of Islamic art.

The Louvre's Islamic Art Exhibit also explores the architectural achievements of the Islamic world, particularly through its collection of architectural fragments, tiles, and models. Islamic architecture is renowned for its innovation and beauty, particularly in the design of mosques, madrasas (religious schools), and palaces. The exhibit includes examples of architectural elements such as carved wooden doors, stucco decorations, and glazed ceramic tiles, many of which were once part of grand buildings in cities like Cairo, Damascus, Isfahan, and Samarkand. One of the most significant architectural pieces in the Louvre's collection is a set of tiles from the Dome of the Rock in Jerusalem, one of the most important and iconic buildings in Islamic history. These tiles, decorated with vibrant geometric patterns and floral motifs, are a testament to the skill of Islamic architects and craftsmen, who combined aesthetic beauty with structural innovation to create buildings that were both functional and spiritually uplifting.

The Louvre's Islamic Art Exhibit is not only a display of beautiful objects but also a journey through the history of the Islamic world, from its early beginnings in the Arabian Peninsula to its expansion across Africa, Asia, and Europe. The exhibit highlights the diversity of Islamic cultures, as each region developed its own unique artistic traditions while also contributing to a shared Islamic aesthetic. It also emphasizes the cross-cultural exchanges that took place between the Islamic world and other civilizations, such as Byzantine, Persian, and European societies. For example, many of the objects in the Louvre's collection, such as ceramics, textiles, and metalwork, show the influence of Chinese, Indian, and Mediterranean art forms, demonstrating the interconnectedness of the medieval world through trade, diplomacy, and conquest.

One of the goals of the Louvre's Islamic Art Exhibit is to foster a deeper understanding and appreciation of Islamic culture and its contributions to global civilization. By presenting Islamic art in a museum setting, the exhibit encourages visitors to see beyond stereotypes and misconceptions, recognizing the complexity, diversity, and beauty of Islamic artistic traditions. The exhibit also highlights the universal themes that connect Islamic art with other artistic traditions, such as the search for beauty, the expression of religious and spiritual values, and the celebration of human creativity.

In conclusion, the Louvre's Islamic Art Exhibit is a remarkable collection that showcases the artistic, cultural, and intellectual achievements of the Islamic world over more than a thousand years. From calligraphy and ceramics to metalwork, glass, and textiles, the objects in this exhibit reflect the diversity and richness of Islamic civilization. The exhibit not only highlights the beauty and craftsmanship of Islamic art but also serves as a reminder of the important role that Islamic culture has played in shaping the history of art and civilization. Visitors to the Louvre's Islamic Art Exhibit are invited to explore this fascinating and often misunderstood world, gaining a deeper appreciation for the creativity, innovation, and spiritual depth of Islamic art.

Chapter 9: The Story of the Winged Victory of Samothrace

The *Winged Victory of Samothrace*, also known as the *Nike of Samothrace*, is one of the most celebrated masterpieces of Hellenistic sculpture and a central attraction at the Louvre Museum in Paris. This awe-inspiring marble statue, representing the Greek goddess Nike (Victory), is both a symbol of triumphant achievement and a remarkable example of the technical skill and artistic sophistication that characterized the art of ancient Greece. The statue, created around 190 BCE, stands as a testament to the ideals of victory and motion, capturing a dynamic moment frozen in time. Its powerful presence, dramatic pose, and exquisite detailing have made it one of the most iconic works of ancient art, admired for its combination of naturalism and idealism.

The statue was discovered on the small island of Samothrace in the northern Aegean Sea in 1863 by the French archaeologist Charles Champoiseau. Samothrace was known in antiquity as the site of an important religious sanctuary dedicated to the gods of the Great Mysteries, a cult associated with the worship of deities related to protection and salvation, particularly in connection with seafaring and naval victories. The *Winged Victory* was originally placed in a prominent location within this sanctuary, atop a cliff overlooking the sea. Its setting, combined with its monumental scale and dramatic composition, would have made it visible from a distance, serving as a powerful symbol of divine intervention and victory in naval warfare.

The exact origins of the statue and the event it was intended to commemorate remain subjects of debate among scholars, but it is widely believed that it was created to celebrate a naval victory, possibly one achieved by the Rhodians, a seafaring people from the island of Rhodes. The connection to naval warfare is further supported by the fact that the *Winged Victory* was originally set atop a sculpted prow of a ship, as if the goddess was descending to land on the deck, bringing divine favor to the victors. The ship's prow, which is part of the base of the sculpture, reinforces the maritime theme, suggesting that the statue was a votive offering made in gratitude for a successful battle at sea. This connection between Nike and naval victory is consistent with the widespread Greek practice of dedicating statues and monuments to the gods in thanksgiving for military successes.

Standing at nearly 8 feet tall (2.44 meters), the *Winged Victory of Samothrace* is a monumental sculpture that exudes energy, movement, and grace. Although the statue is missing its head and arms, the remaining figure is a masterpiece of Hellenistic art, a period known for its emphasis on realism, drama, and emotional intensity. The statue depicts Nike as she descends from the heavens, her wings outstretched and her body twisting slightly to one side as if she has just alighted on the prow of a ship. The dynamic pose, with one foot forward and her torso slightly turned, conveys a sense of forward momentum, as though she is about to take another step. The positioning of her wings, which appear to have just caught the wind, further enhances the impression of movement, giving the sculpture a sense of immediacy and vitality.

One of the most striking features of the *Winged Victory of Samothrace* is the skillful rendering of the drapery that clings to the goddess's body. The thin, flowing fabric of her garment, known as a chiton, is depicted with remarkable precision, its folds and pleats rippling across her figure as if they are being blown by the sea breeze. The drapery both conceals and reveals the underlying structure of her body, emphasizing her physical strength and grace. The way the fabric clings to her torso and legs creates a sense of tension, as though the wind is pressing it against her, while the loose folds around her waist and arms give the sculpture a sense of lightness and fluidity. This treatment of drapery is a hallmark of Hellenistic sculpture, which sought to combine naturalism with idealized beauty, capturing both the physical and emotional qualities of the subject.

The missing head and arms of the *Winged Victory of Samothrace* have sparked much speculation and reconstruction efforts. Scholars believe that her right arm was originally raised, perhaps holding a laurel wreath or a palm branch—both traditional symbols of victory in Greek art. The gesture of Nike raising her arm to crown the victors would have added to the statue's overall message of triumph and divine approval. While the loss of the head might seem like a significant drawback, the statue's power and dynamism are not diminished by its incomplete state. In fact, the absence of these parts has contributed to the statue's mystique, allowing viewers to focus on the sweeping movement of the body and wings.

The *Winged Victory of Samothrace* was designed not only to be a standalone work of art but also to interact with its environment in a very deliberate way. The statue's original placement in the Sanctuary of the Great Gods on Samothrace would have been carefully chosen to heighten its visual impact. Positioned on a terrace that overlooked the sea, the statue would have appeared to be emerging from the landscape, with the wind-swept drapery and wings enhancing the illusion of flight. The interplay between the statue, the surrounding natural environment, and the distant view of the sea would have created a dramatic and awe-inspiring effect, reinforcing the idea of Nike as a powerful divine force capable of intervening in human affairs.

After its discovery in 1863, the *Winged Victory of Samothrace* was transported to Paris, where it was eventually placed in the Louvre Museum. Over time, it became one of the museum's most popular and beloved pieces, celebrated for its artistic excellence and emotional power. The statue was initially displayed in various locations within the Louvre, but in 1883, it was installed at the top of the grand Daru staircase, where it remains to this day. This location, one of the most prominent spots in the museum, allows visitors to experience the statue from multiple angles and appreciate its commanding presence. The positioning of the *Winged Victory* at the top of the staircase also echoes its original placement in the Sanctuary of the Great Gods, where it was similarly elevated to overlook its surroundings.

In addition to its aesthetic and historical significance, the *Winged Victory of Samothrace* has come to symbolize a variety of cultural and ideological values over the years. For many, the statue represents not only military victory but also the triumph of human achievement and artistic excellence. The figure of Nike, descending from the heavens to bestow victory upon the deserving, can be seen as a metaphor for the pursuit of excellence, both in art and in life. The dynamic movement of the statue, combined with the goddess's sense of purpose and power, has made it a symbol of ambition, progress, and determination. In this sense, the *Winged Victory* has transcended its original context as a monument to a specific naval victory and has become a universal symbol of success, aspiration, and the human spirit.

Over the centuries, the *Winged Victory of Samothrace* has also exerted a profound influence on artists, writers, and thinkers. Its dramatic pose, sense of movement, and idealized beauty have inspired numerous artists, from the neoclassical sculptors of the 18th and 19th centuries to modern and contemporary creators. The statue's combination of realism and abstraction, with its lifelike depiction of the human form juxtaposed with its missing head and arms, has sparked debates about the nature of art, beauty, and the representation of the human body. For many modern artists, the *Winged Victory* represents the tension between perfection and imperfection, between the ideal and the real, making it a source of endless fascination and interpretation.

In the 20th century, the *Winged Victory of Samothrace* took on new symbolic meanings in the context of global conflicts and the fight for freedom. During World War II, the statue was moved from the Louvre to a safe location to protect it from potential damage during the German occupation of France. Its survival through the war became a symbol of resilience and endurance, representing the triumph of cultural heritage and human creativity over the forces of destruction and oppression. In the postwar era, the *Winged Victory* has continued to be associated with ideas of peace, freedom, and human dignity, standing as a reminder of the enduring power of art to inspire and uplift.

The technical mastery involved in creating the *Winged Victory of Samothrace* is another aspect that has long fascinated scholars and artists alike. The statue is carved from Parian marble, a fine-grained white marble prized by ancient sculptors for its translucency and ability to hold intricate details. The sculptor's ability to capture the delicate texture of the goddess's skin, the soft folds of her garments, and the feathered intricacy of her wings is a testament to the high level of skill and craftsmanship that characterized Hellenistic sculpture. The choice of marble also reflects the importance of the statue as a religious and commemorative monument, as marble was often reserved for the most prestigious and sacred works of art.

The restoration of the *Winged Victory of Samothrace* over the years has provided new insights into the original appearance of the statue and its significance in ancient Greek culture. In the late 19th century, French archaeologists uncovered additional fragments of the statue, including parts of the ship's prow and fragments of the wings. These discoveries allowed for a more accurate reconstruction of the statue's original context and appearance. In 2013, the Louvre undertook a major restoration project to clean and conserve the statue, revealing new details about the surface of the marble and the techniques used by the ancient sculptor. The restoration also improved the stability of the statue, ensuring that it can continue to inspire future generations of visitors.

In conclusion, the *Winged Victory of Samothrace* is a masterpiece of ancient Greek art that continues to captivate and inspire audiences around the world. Its dynamic pose, intricate detailing, and symbolic power make it one of the most remarkable examples of Hellenistic sculpture. The statue's representation of the goddess Nike, descending to bestow victory, speaks to the ideals of triumph, achievement, and divine favor that were central to Greek culture. Although it was created to commemorate a specific naval victory, the *Winged Victory* has transcended its original context to become a universal symbol of success, ambition, and the human spirit. Whether viewed as an artistic masterpiece, a historical artifact, or a cultural icon, the *Winged Victory of Samothrace* remains one of the most enduring and powerful works of art in human history. Its placement at the top of the Daru staircase in the Louvre allows it to preside over the museum as a beacon of inspiration, inviting visitors to marvel at its beauty and to reflect on the timeless values of creativity, excellence, and victory that it embodies.

Chapter 10: The Louvre During the French Revolution

The French Revolution, a period of radical social and political upheaval that began in 1789, had a profound impact on the Louvre, transforming it from a royal palace into one of the most famous museums in the world. Before the Revolution, the Louvre had been a symbol of royal power and authority, serving as a residence for French kings and as a repository for the art and cultural treasures of the monarchy. However, as the Revolution gained momentum, the role of the Louvre shifted dramatically. The Revolutionaries, driven by ideals of equality, citizenship, and public ownership of national treasures, sought to open the royal collections to the people. This transformation of the Louvre from an exclusive royal domain into a public museum was not only a reflection of the political changes occurring in France but also a key moment in the democratization of art and culture.

Before the French Revolution, the Louvre had a long history as a royal residence. Originally built as a fortress in the late 12th century by King Philip II to protect Paris from invasions, it was gradually transformed into a royal palace over the centuries. By the 16th century, King Francis I began using the Louvre as a residence and filled it with art and treasures, laying the foundation for the royal art collection that would later become the core of the Louvre Museum. The kings who followed, particularly Louis XIV, continued to expand the collection, acquiring masterpieces from across Europe. However, during Louis XIV's reign, the court moved to the Palace of Versailles, leaving the Louvre primarily as a storage space for royal art rather than an active royal residence.

The Revolution, which began in 1789, drastically altered the political and social landscape of France, and the Louvre was not immune to these changes. In the early years of the Revolution, as the monarchy crumbled and France underwent rapid and often violent transformation, there was a growing sentiment among Revolutionaries that the royal art collection should belong to the people rather than to the monarchy. The National Assembly, the revolutionary government, began to advocate for the nationalization of the royal art collection and the establishment of a public museum. This idea was closely aligned with the Enlightenment ideals that had inspired the Revolution, particularly the belief that knowledge, art, and culture should be accessible to all citizens, not just the privileged elite.

In 1791, a major step was taken when the National Assembly decreed that the Louvre should be transformed into a museum "for the benefit of the people," symbolizing the shift from monarchy to republic and from private ownership to public access. This decision marked the beginning of the Louvre's journey as a public institution, dedicated to the education and cultural enrichment of all citizens. The transformation of the Louvre was not simply a physical change but also a symbolic one. It represented the Revolution's desire to break with the old order and to create a new society based on the principles of equality and civic responsibility. By opening the Louvre to the public, the Revolutionaries sought to promote the idea that art and culture were not the exclusive domain of the aristocracy but a shared national heritage that belonged to everyone.

The opening of the Louvre as a public museum officially took place on August 10, 1793, the first anniversary of the fall of the monarchy. This date was highly symbolic, as it marked the moment when King Louis XVI had been deposed, signaling the end of centuries of royal rule. The decision to open the Louvre to the public on this particular date underscored the Revolutionaries' desire to create a new cultural order in which the people, rather than the king, were the ultimate authority. The museum, which was initially called the *Musée Central des Arts*, was opened in the Grande Galerie, a long, light-filled hall that had been part of the royal palace. The opening exhibition featured a selection of the finest works from the royal collection, including masterpieces by artists such as Raphael, Veronese, and Poussin, many of which had previously been accessible only to the king and his court.

The early years of the Louvre as a public museum were marked by both enthusiasm and challenges. The Revolutionaries were eager to demonstrate that the museum was a public institution, open to all citizens, regardless of class or social status. Admission to the museum was free, and visitors from all walks of life were encouraged to come and appreciate the treasures that had once been the exclusive property of the monarchy. The museum became a symbol of the Revolution's commitment to education and culture, as well as a tool for promoting civic pride and national unity. However, the transition from royal palace to public museum was not without difficulties. The Revolutionary government was struggling with financial instability, political upheaval, and internal conflict, which made it difficult to maintain the museum's collections and infrastructure.

One of the most pressing issues facing the newly established Louvre Museum was the care and conservation of the artworks. The revolutionary fervor that had swept through France in the early 1790s had led to widespread destruction of religious and royal property, including art and cultural artifacts. Churches, monasteries, and aristocratic estates were looted or vandalized, and many valuable works of art were damaged or lost. In response, the Revolutionary government implemented measures to protect France's artistic heritage by confiscating works of art from churches, monasteries, and aristocratic collections and transferring them to the Louvre. This process of "nationalization" dramatically expanded the museum's collection, as thousands of works were brought in from across the country. These confiscations were justified on the grounds that the artworks were part of the national heritage and should be preserved for the benefit of all citizens.

The Revolutionaries also recognized the need for experts to oversee the management and preservation of the Louvre's collections. In 1793, a committee of curators and artists, known as the *Commission des Arts*, was established to organize the museum and ensure the proper care of the artworks. The commission was responsible for cataloging the collection, curating exhibitions, and developing guidelines for the restoration and preservation of the artworks. Notably, the commission included prominent artists and intellectuals, such as Jacques-Louis David, a leading painter of the Revolution, who played a key role in shaping the museum's vision and policies. David, along with other members of the commission, saw the museum as an educational tool that could inspire citizens with the values of the Revolution, particularly patriotism, civic virtue, and a sense of collective ownership of the nation's cultural heritage.

Despite these efforts, the Louvre faced considerable challenges during the turbulent years of the Revolution. The museum was often understaffed, underfunded, and plagued by political instability. The revolutionary government, embroiled in wars with foreign powers and internal strife, struggled to provide adequate resources for the museum's upkeep. Many of the works of art were in poor condition due to neglect, damage, or improper storage, and the museum's facilities were not always sufficient to protect the delicate paintings, sculptures, and artifacts. Moreover, the political climate of the Revolution was highly volatile, and the museum's administrators had to navigate shifting alliances, power struggles, and ideological conflicts. At times, the museum itself became a political battleground, as different factions sought to impose their own vision of what the museum should represent.

One of the most dramatic episodes in the Louvre's history during the Revolution occurred in 1794, during the Reign of Terror, a period of intense political repression and violence led by the radical Jacobins. Under the leadership of Maximilien Robespierre, the Revolutionary government intensified its efforts to purge France of perceived enemies, including members of the aristocracy, clergy, and political rivals. During this time, the Louvre came under scrutiny, as some Revolutionary leaders viewed the museum's collection as a remnant of the old regime that needed to be reformed or purged of its royalist and religious associations. However, cooler heads prevailed, and the Louvre was spared from the destruction that befell many other cultural institutions during the Reign of Terror. In fact, the museum continued to grow during this period, as more artworks were confiscated and added to its collection.

The Louvre's transformation into a museum during the Revolution also reflected broader changes in the way art was viewed and understood in French society. Before the Revolution, art had primarily been associated with the monarchy, the church, and the aristocracy, serving as a symbol of power, wealth, and status. However, the Revolutionaries sought to redefine the role of art, emphasizing its educational and moral value rather than its association with privilege and elitism. Art was seen as a tool for promoting civic virtue, patriotism, and moral instruction. The Louvre, as a public museum, was intended to serve as a space where citizens could learn about history, culture, and the values of the Republic. The museum's collection was curated to reflect these ideals, with an emphasis on works that depicted themes of heroism, sacrifice, and virtue, as well as scenes from classical mythology, history, and the Revolution itself.

The Louvre's collection continued to grow throughout the Revolution, thanks in large part to the military campaigns of the Revolutionary and Napoleonic armies. As French forces conquered territories across Europe, they often seized works of art from the cities they occupied, bringing them back to France as trophies of war. Napoleon Bonaparte, who rose to power in the late 1790s, was particularly enthusiastic about expanding the Louvre's collection. He viewed the museum as a symbol of France's cultural supremacy and sought to fill it with the finest works of art from across Europe. During his campaigns in Italy, the Netherlands, and elsewhere, Napoleon's troops looted churches, palaces, and museums, sending back countless masterpieces, including works by artists such as Leonardo da Vinci, Raphael, and Titian. These looted treasures further enriched the Louvre's collection and cemented its status as one of the greatest museums in the world.

The Louvre's transformation during the French Revolution had a lasting impact on the institution and on the broader world of art and culture. By turning the royal palace into a public museum, the Revolutionaries set a precedent for the democratization of art, making it accessible to all citizens rather than keeping it as the exclusive domain of the elite. The creation of the Louvre as a public museum also helped to establish the modern concept of the museum as a space for education, civic engagement, and the preservation of cultural heritage. The Louvre's success inspired the creation of other public museums across Europe and around the world, contributing to a broader movement toward the public ownership and display of art.

In conclusion, the French Revolution was a pivotal moment in the history of the Louvre, transforming it from a royal palace into a public museum that symbolized the new ideals of the Republic. The Louvre's transition during this period reflected the Revolution's broader goals of equality, citizenship, and public access to culture. Despite the challenges and political turmoil of the Revolution, the museum grew in size and importance, becoming a central institution in French cultural life. The Louvre's evolution during the Revolution also had a profound influence on the development of modern museums, helping to shape the idea of art as a public good and a national treasure. Today, the Louvre stands as a testament to the enduring legacy of the French Revolution and the power of art to inspire, educate, and unite people across time and space.

Chapter 11: Napoleon's Influence on the Louvre

Napoleon Bonaparte's influence on the Louvre is monumental, shaping its transformation from a nascent public museum into one of the most celebrated and iconic cultural institutions in the world. When Napoleon rose to power in the late 18th century, the Louvre had only recently been converted from a royal palace to a public museum, a change initiated by the French Revolution. While the Revolutionary leaders laid the foundation for the museum's opening, it was under Napoleon's rule that the Louvre truly expanded and evolved into a world-class institution. Napoleon's military conquests, ambitious cultural vision, and strategic use of art as a tool of political propaganda significantly increased the Louvre's collection, bringing in masterpieces from across Europe and turning the museum into a symbol of French cultural supremacy.

Before Napoleon came to power, the Louvre was opened as a public museum in 1793 during the French Revolution. The idea behind its opening was to make art accessible to all citizens, symbolizing the end of monarchy and aristocratic privilege. However, the museum's collection at that time was primarily limited to the royal art collection, consisting of works that had been accumulated over centuries by the French monarchy. While the Revolutionary government did confiscate artworks from churches, monasteries, and aristocratic estates, the Louvre's collection was still relatively modest compared to the vast holdings it would acquire under Napoleon.

Napoleon, who seized power through a coup d'état in 1799, saw art and culture as essential components of his broader political and military ambitions. He viewed the Louvre not only as a public museum but also as a tool for enhancing his own prestige and for reinforcing his image as a leader of both military genius and cultural patronage.

Art, in Napoleon's mind, was not merely a passive display of beauty but a powerful symbol of national pride, intellectual superiority, and political dominance. Through his policies and military conquests, Napoleon transformed the Louvre into a repository of the finest treasures of European civilization, many of which were seized from the nations he conquered.

Napoleon's military campaigns across Europe, often referred to as the Napoleonic Wars, played a central role in expanding the Louvre's collection. As his armies advanced through Italy, the Netherlands, Austria, Spain, and other territories, they systematically looted artworks from churches, palaces, and museums, often under the guise of treaties or cultural exchange. These seizures were justified by Napoleon's administration as acts of reparation or as rewards for France's military victories. For Napoleon, bringing these works of art back to France was a way to demonstrate the cultural and intellectual superiority of the French nation. By filling the Louvre with treasures from across Europe, Napoleon sought to turn Paris into the cultural capital of the world and to assert France's dominance in both military and artistic spheres.

One of the most famous examples of Napoleon's art looting occurred during his Italian campaign in the late 1790s. After defeating the armies of the Papal States and other Italian territories, Napoleon forced their rulers to sign treaties that included clauses requiring the surrender of important works of art to France. These treaties, such as the Treaty of Tolentino (1797) with the Papal States, allowed Napoleon to claim countless masterpieces as spoils of war. Some of the most significant works acquired during this period included the *Apollo Belvedere* and the *Laocoön* group, both of which had been housed in the Vatican collections. These ancient sculptures, considered among the greatest achievements of classical art, were triumphantly transported to Paris and placed in the Louvre, where they became symbols of France's newfound cultural dominance.

The Italian campaigns also brought several of Leonardo da Vinci's masterpieces into the Louvre's collection. Among the most famous works acquired during this period was *The Last Supper*, which was taken from the refectory of the Convent of Santa Maria delle Grazie in Milan. Although this fragile mural could not be physically moved to Paris, other significant works by Leonardo, such as his celebrated paintings *Saint John the Baptist* and *The Virgin and Child with Saint Anne*, were added to the Louvre's collection, further enhancing its reputation as a repository of the finest European art.

Napoleon's looting extended beyond Italy. During his campaigns in the Netherlands, he seized numerous paintings by Flemish and Dutch masters, including works by Peter Paul Rubens, Anthony van Dyck, and Rembrandt. These acquisitions further enriched the Louvre's collection, particularly in the field of Northern European painting. Rubens' *Marie de' Medici Cycle*, a series of 24 monumental paintings originally commissioned for the Luxembourg Palace in Paris, was one of the most significant additions to the museum during this period. The series, which depicts the life of Marie de' Medici, Queen of France, is renowned for its dynamic composition, vibrant color, and intricate detail, and it became a centerpiece of the Louvre's collection of Baroque art.

Napoleon's expansionist ambitions reached their zenith with his invasion of Egypt in 1798. Although the Egyptian campaign was ultimately a military failure, it had significant cultural ramifications, particularly for the Louvre. The French army included a group of scholars and scientists known as the *Commission des Sciences et des Arts*, who were tasked with documenting and studying the rich history and culture of Egypt. Their efforts led to the discovery of many ancient artifacts, including the famous *Rosetta Stone*, which played a crucial role in deciphering Egyptian hieroglyphs. While the *Rosetta Stone* eventually ended up in the British Museum following Napoleon's defeat in Egypt, other Egyptian artifacts were brought back to France and added to the Louvre's collection. This marked the beginning of the museum's renowned Egyptian collection, which continues to be one of the largest and most important collections of Egyptian antiquities in the world.

Napoleon's influence on the Louvre extended beyond the mere acquisition of art. He also undertook significant architectural and organizational changes to the museum itself. In 1803, Napoleon renamed the Louvre the *Musée Napoléon*, a symbolic gesture that underscored the close association between the museum and his regime. Under his direction, the museum was reorganized and expanded to accommodate the growing collection of artworks. He appointed Dominique Vivant Denon, an artist, archaeologist, and diplomat, as the museum's first director. Denon, who had accompanied Napoleon on the Egyptian campaign and shared his passion for art, played a key role in shaping the Louvre's identity during the Napoleonic era. Under Denon's leadership, the Louvre became more systematically organized, with collections arranged by school and period, making it easier for visitors to navigate and appreciate the museum's vast holdings.

Napoleon also initiated a series of grand architectural projects designed to enhance the Louvre's status as a cultural and political symbol. One of his most ambitious plans was to connect the Louvre with the nearby Tuileries Palace, creating a unified complex that would serve as both a museum and a royal residence. While this project was never fully completed, it laid the groundwork for the eventual expansion of the Louvre in the 19th century. Napoleon's vision for the museum as a symbol of French greatness also extended to its public image. He frequently hosted grand receptions and exhibitions at the Louvre, using the museum as a backdrop for displays of imperial power and cultural prestige. These events were designed to impress foreign dignitaries and to reinforce Napoleon's image as a patron of the arts and a leader of unparalleled vision.

Despite the vast expansion of the Louvre's collection during Napoleon's reign, his legacy at the museum is not without controversy. Much of the art that was brought to the Louvre during this period was acquired through force, often at the expense of other nations' cultural heritage. After Napoleon's defeat at the Battle of Waterloo in 1815 and the subsequent fall of his empire, many of the works of art that had been looted from other countries were returned to their original owners as part of the peace settlements. The *Congress of Vienna* and the *Treaty of Paris* both stipulated the restitution of many of the artworks that had been seized by Napoleon's armies. This resulted in the return of countless masterpieces to Italy, the Netherlands, Austria, and other nations, a process that significantly diminished the Louvre's collection. For example, the *Apollo Belvedere* and the *Laocoön* group were both returned to the Vatican, while many of Rubens' paintings were sent back to Belgium.

However, not all of the artworks that were taken by Napoleon's forces were returned, and some of the pieces acquired during his reign remain in the Louvre to this day. Additionally, even after the restitution of many works, the Louvre's collection was still significantly larger than it had been before Napoleon's conquests. The museum had acquired a level of prestige and international recognition that it had not previously enjoyed, and it remained one of the most important cultural institutions in the world. The Napoleonic era also left a lasting legacy in terms of the Louvre's organization, architecture, and mission as a public museum.

In conclusion, Napoleon's influence on the Louvre was profound and far-reaching. Through his military conquests, he dramatically expanded the museum's collection, bringing in masterpieces from across Europe and turning the Louvre into a symbol of French cultural supremacy. His ambitious vision for the museum, both as a repository of art and as a symbol of imperial power, helped to shape the Louvre's identity as one of the world's greatest museums. Although many of the works acquired during Napoleon's reign were later returned to their original countries, his legacy at the Louvre endures. The museum's vast collection, its architectural grandeur, and its status as a global cultural icon all owe a significant debt to Napoleon's influence. Today, the Louvre stands not only as a testament to the power of art but also as a reminder of the complex relationship between politics, culture, and empire.

Chapter 12: Exploring the Louvre's Medieval Fortress

Exploring the Louvre's medieval fortress takes visitors back to a time before the grand palace and world-renowned museum stood on the banks of the Seine. Long before it became the symbol of art, culture, and luxury that it is today, the Louvre was a formidable fortress built to protect Paris from potential invasions. This period in the Louvre's history is not only fascinating but also sheds light on the very origins of the structure that would evolve into one of the most famous museums in the world. Understanding the Louvre's medieval roots allows us to appreciate the transformation from its defensive function to its later use as a royal palace and, eventually, a cultural institution.

The story of the Louvre as a fortress begins in the late 12th century under the reign of King Philip II of France. At this time, Paris was an important but vulnerable city, surrounded by hostile forces and prone to attack. Philip, often called Philip Augustus, recognized the need to protect his capital from foreign invasions, particularly those from the English, who had significant territories in France. In response to these threats, Philip decided to construct a series of fortifications around Paris, with the Louvre fortress being one of the key elements of this defensive strategy.

The construction of the Louvre fortress began around 1190, and its purpose was purely military. Located on the western edge of medieval Paris, the fortress was strategically placed along the banks of the Seine River to guard against invasions that might come from the river or from the surrounding countryside. At the time, this location was on the outskirts of the city, far from the bustling heart of medieval Paris, and it served as both a defensive stronghold and a royal armory.

The original design of the Louvre fortress was typical of medieval military architecture, with high, thick walls, fortified towers, and a deep moat. The most distinctive feature of the fortress was its large, circular keep, known as the *donjon*. The keep was the strongest part of the fortress and served as the last line of defense in the event of an attack. Standing at the center of the complex, the keep was surrounded by a rectangular curtain wall with ten defensive towers positioned along its perimeter. These towers were equipped with battlements, arrow slits, and other defensive features that allowed the defenders to repel attackers while remaining protected.

The keep itself was an imposing structure, rising nearly 30 meters high and built from thick stone blocks. Inside, it housed the royal treasury, archives, and a small garrison of soldiers who were responsible for defending the fortress. The walls of the keep were so thick that they could withstand prolonged sieges, and the entire structure was designed to be self-sufficient in case the surrounding areas fell to enemy forces. The fortress also included living quarters for the soldiers, storage rooms for weapons and supplies, and dungeons for prisoners. While it was primarily a military installation, the fortress also had a symbolic role, representing the king's authority and power in a turbulent and often dangerous time.

For nearly two centuries, the Louvre served as one of the key defensive structures protecting Paris. However, as the city grew and expanded beyond its original walls, the role of the Louvre began to change. By the 14th century, Paris had outgrown the medieval fortifications built by Philip Augustus, and new walls were constructed farther out to protect the enlarged city. As a result, the Louvre fortress lost much of its military significance and was no longer needed as a frontline defense against foreign invasions. However, it remained an important royal residence and continued to house the king's treasury, as well as serving as a prison and a military arsenal.

The transformation of the Louvre from a fortress into a royal residence began in earnest in the 14th century under the reign of King Charles V of France. Charles, who ruled from 1364 to 1380, decided to convert the fortress into a more comfortable and luxurious residence fit for a king. The keep, which had once been a symbol of military power, was renovated to include grand living quarters, reception rooms, and private chambers for the king and his court. Charles also added gardens, courtyards, and a chapel, transforming the fortress into a palace while still maintaining many of its defensive features. Despite these renovations, the Louvre retained much of its medieval character, and its massive walls, towers, and moats remained a prominent feature of the Parisian landscape.

In the centuries that followed, the Louvre continued to evolve, as successive kings added their own architectural innovations and expansions to the complex. However, the fortress's military origins were never entirely erased. Even as the Louvre became a grand royal palace, elements of its medieval past remained visible. The old keep and portions of the original walls and towers survived well into the Renaissance, serving as a reminder of the Louvre's defensive role in the history of Paris.

The most significant changes to the Louvre came in the 16th century under King Francis I, who began the process of turning the medieval fortress into a Renaissance palace. Francis, a great patron of the arts, initiated a major renovation and expansion project that included the demolition of the old keep and the construction of the Renaissance-style wings that are now associated with the Louvre. While much of the original fortress was dismantled during this period, some of the medieval elements were preserved or incorporated into the new palace design. For example, the medieval moat was kept intact, and parts of the old walls were integrated into the new construction.

By the time of Louis XIV's reign in the 17th century, the Louvre had completely transitioned from a fortress to a royal palace, and the medieval defensive structures had largely disappeared from view. The palace became the official residence of the French monarchy, and its role as a symbol of royal power and cultural prestige overshadowed its earlier military function. However, the Louvre's medieval history was not entirely forgotten, and traces of the original fortress remained hidden beneath the surface, waiting to be rediscovered.

The rediscovery of the Louvre's medieval past came centuries later, in the 1980s, during a massive renovation project known as the *Grand Louvre*. This ambitious project, initiated by French President François Mitterrand, aimed to modernize the museum and expand its exhibition space. During the excavations for the project, archaeologists uncovered the remains of the original medieval fortress, including sections of the walls, towers, and the base of the keep. These discoveries were a revelation, offering a glimpse into a long-forgotten chapter of the Louvre's history.

Today, visitors to the Louvre can explore the remains of the medieval fortress in the *Sully Wing*, where parts of the original structure have been preserved and are on display. The most impressive of these remains is the massive foundation of the keep, which is now located in the museum's basement. Visitors can walk through the old moat and see the thick stone walls that once formed the heart of the fortress. The scale of the keep's foundation gives a sense of the sheer size and strength of the original structure, highlighting its role as a formidable defensive installation.

In addition to the keep, other features of the medieval fortress can be seen in the *Medieval Louvre* exhibit, which includes a section of the fortress wall, a defensive tower, and parts of the moat. The exhibit also features artifacts from the medieval period, including weapons, armor, and everyday objects used by the soldiers who once garrisoned the fortress. These displays offer visitors a deeper understanding of what life was like in the fortress during the Middle Ages, as well as how the building evolved over time.

The preservation of these medieval remains is not only a testament to the historical importance of the Louvre but also a reminder of how the building's function has changed over the centuries. From a fortress designed to defend Paris from external threats to a royal palace that symbolized the power and grandeur of the French monarchy, and finally to a museum that houses some of the world's greatest artistic treasures, the Louvre has undergone a remarkable transformation. However, the presence of the medieval ruins beneath the museum serves as a reminder of its origins as a fortress and of the long history of Paris itself.

Exploring the Louvre's medieval fortress allows visitors to connect with a time when Paris was a smaller, more vulnerable city, and the threat of invasion was a constant concern. The fortress represents a period in history when architecture was as much about defense as it was about grandeur. While today's Louvre is known for its vast art collections and elegant architecture, its medieval origins reveal a different side of its story—a story of kings, soldiers, and the challenges of defending a city on the rise.

The medieval fortress of the Louvre also provides a fascinating contrast to the museum's later developments, particularly the glass pyramid entrance that now dominates the courtyard. The juxtaposition of the ancient stone walls of the fortress with the modern, futuristic design of the pyramid highlights the Louvre's evolution over time, from a medieval stronghold to a cutting-edge cultural institution. This contrast between old and new is a key part of what makes the Louvre such a unique and compelling destination. It is not just a museum of art but a living monument to the history of Paris and France, with layers of history that span nearly a thousand years.

In conclusion, the exploration of the Louvre's medieval fortress offers a deep dive into the building's earliest days as a defensive stronghold. The transformation from a fortress protecting Paris to a palace and then a museum reflects the broader history of France itself. Today, the preserved remnants of the medieval structure provide a tangible link to the past, allowing visitors to experience a time when the Louvre was more about walls and moats than paintings and sculptures.

This chapter of the Louvre's history, often overshadowed by its later role as a royal palace and museum, is a critical part of understanding the full story of one of the world's most famous buildings. Exploring the medieval fortress within the Louvre is like stepping into another era, one filled with knights, kings, and the ever-present threat of war, a far cry from the peaceful halls that now house some of humanity's greatest artistic achievements.

Chapter 13: The Famous Venus de Milo Statue

The Venus de Milo is one of the most celebrated and enigmatic sculptures in the history of art, captivating millions of visitors who flock to the Louvre Museum each year. This stunning marble statue, believed to represent Aphrodite, the Greek goddess of love and beauty, stands as a testament to the artistry of ancient Greece and the timeless allure of classical sculpture. Despite being more than 2,000 years old, the Venus de Milo continues to inspire awe, curiosity, and debate over its origins, its missing arms, and its meaning. As one of the Louvre's most famous masterpieces, the Venus de Milo holds a place not only in the annals of art history but also in popular culture, symbolizing both the ideal of beauty and the mystery of antiquity.

The story of the Venus de Milo begins in the ancient world, though much about the statue's early history remains shrouded in uncertainty. The sculpture was discovered in 1820 on the island of Milos, in the Aegean Sea, by a Greek farmer named Yorgos Kentrotas. According to accounts, Kentrotas stumbled upon the statue while digging in the ruins of an ancient city on the island. The statue was found in pieces, partially buried in the ground, but it was clear from the moment of its discovery that it was an extraordinary work of art. Its exquisite craftsmanship, smooth marble surface, and graceful pose immediately suggested that it was the creation of a master sculptor from ancient Greece.

The exact origins of the Venus de Milo, including its creator and the time of its creation, remain topics of scholarly debate. Art historians generally agree that the statue dates back to between 130 and 100 BCE, during the Hellenistic period, a time when Greek art had reached its height in terms of technical skill and naturalistic representation. The Hellenistic era was marked by an emphasis on dynamic movement, emotion, and realism in sculpture, as opposed to the more restrained and idealized forms of earlier periods of Greek art. The Venus de Milo reflects these stylistic trends, with its flowing drapery and subtly twisted torso suggesting a sense of movement and life, even as the figure stands in a relaxed, almost serene pose.

While the Venus de Milo is often associated with the classical Greek sculptor Praxiteles, who was famous for his depictions of Aphrodite, there is no definitive evidence to confirm the identity of the statue's creator. Some scholars have proposed that it was sculpted by Alexandros of Antioch, an artist who worked in the late Hellenistic period, based on an inscription found near the statue that seems to mention his name. However, the inscription is incomplete, and the attribution remains speculative. Regardless of its creator, the Venus de Milo is widely regarded as one of the greatest achievements of Greek sculpture, a work that epitomizes the beauty and elegance of the human form.

The subject of the Venus de Milo has also been a matter of debate, though it is generally accepted that the statue represents Aphrodite, known as Venus in Roman mythology. The goddess of love and beauty was a popular subject in ancient Greek art, and many statues of her were created during the Hellenistic period. The Venus de Milo, with its graceful proportions, soft curves, and sensual drapery, seems to embody the classical ideal of feminine beauty that was central to Greek depictions of Aphrodite. The statue's partially nude form, with the upper body exposed and the lower half covered by a flowing garment, is typical of Hellenistic representations of the goddess, which often emphasized both her divinity and her sensuality.

One of the most striking aspects of the Venus de Milo is its missing arms, a feature that has contributed significantly to the statue's mystique and fame. When the statue was discovered, its arms were already missing, and despite extensive efforts to recover them, they have never been found. The absence of the arms has sparked endless speculation about how the statue originally looked and what the figure might have been doing. Some art historians believe that the statue was holding an apple in one hand, a reference to the mythological story of the Judgment of Paris, in which Aphrodite was awarded a golden apple for being the most beautiful of the goddesses. Others suggest that the statue may have held a mirror, a common attribute of Aphrodite in ancient art, or that she was leaning on a column or shield.

The lack of arms has also raised questions about the posture and balance of the figure. The Venus de Milo's torso is subtly twisted, with the weight of the body shifted onto the right leg, a pose known as *contrapposto*, which was favored by ancient Greek sculptors for its naturalism and grace. This twist of the body, combined with the flowing drapery, creates a sense of dynamic movement, as if the figure is caught in a moment of action. Some scholars have argued that the missing arms were essential to the overall composition of the statue, helping to balance the figure and enhance the sense of movement. Without the arms, the Venus de Milo appears incomplete, and yet it is this very incompleteness that has become a central part of its allure. The missing arms leave room for interpretation and imagination, allowing viewers to project their own ideas about what the figure was doing and what the statue might have originally represented.

The Venus de Milo's journey from its discovery on the island of Milos to its place of honor in the Louvre is a fascinating tale of international intrigue and cultural diplomacy. Shortly after its discovery in 1820, the statue came to the attention of a French naval officer named Olivier Voutier, who was stationed on Milos at the time. Recognizing the importance of the statue, Voutier alerted the French authorities, and negotiations were quickly undertaken to acquire the sculpture for France. At the time, France was still recovering from the Napoleonic Wars, and the acquisition of the Venus de Milo was seen as a way to restore the nation's cultural prestige. The French government arranged for the statue to be transported to Paris, where it was presented to King Louis XVIII and eventually placed in the Louvre.

The acquisition of the Venus de Milo was not without controversy. The Ottoman Empire, which controlled the island of Milos at the time, also laid claim to the statue, and there were disputes over who had the right to possess it. However, through a combination of diplomatic negotiations and French influence in the region, the statue was successfully brought to France, where it was celebrated as a national treasure. Upon its arrival in Paris, the Venus de Milo was immediately hailed as one of the greatest masterpieces of ancient art, and it quickly became one of the Louvre's most prized possessions.

Over the centuries, the Venus de Milo has become an icon of beauty, elegance, and classical art. Its fame has grown to such an extent that it is now one of the most recognizable works of art in the world, often reproduced in textbooks, posters, and popular media. The statue has also inspired countless artists, writers, and poets, who have been captivated by its mysterious beauty and its air of timeless grace. In the 19th and early 20th centuries, the Venus de Milo became a symbol of the neoclassical movement in art, as artists sought to emulate the idealized forms and harmonious proportions of ancient Greek sculpture.

The Venus de Milo's influence extends beyond the world of art. The statue has been referenced in literature, music, film, and even advertising, becoming a cultural touchstone that represents not only beauty but also the enduring power of the classical tradition. In popular culture, the Venus de Milo is often associated with the idea of perfection, despite—or perhaps because of—its missing arms. The statue's incomplete state has led some to view it as a symbol of lost beauty or the fragility of human existence, while others see it as a reminder of the passage of time and the inevitability of decay. Yet, even in its damaged state, the Venus de Milo continues to embody the ideals of balance, harmony, and proportion that have defined classical art for millennia.

The Venus de Milo's presence in the Louvre has only enhanced its reputation as a masterpiece of world art. The statue is displayed in the museum's *Sully Wing*, in a prominent position that allows visitors to view it from multiple angles and appreciate the full scope of its beauty. The setting of the statue, surrounded by other masterpieces of ancient Greek and Roman art, underscores its importance within the broader context of classical sculpture. Visitors to the Louvre are often struck by the sheer size and grandeur of the Venus de Milo, which stands over six feet tall and commands attention with its imposing yet graceful form. The statue's serene expression, flowing drapery, and balanced posture evoke a sense of timelessness and perfection, qualities that have made it a symbol of the Louvre itself.

In conclusion, the Venus de Milo is much more than just a beautiful statue. It is a work of art that encapsulates the ideals of ancient Greek sculpture, a symbol of classical beauty and mystery, and a cultural icon that has captured the imagination of people around the world for centuries. From its origins on the island of Milos to its place in the Louvre, the Venus de Milo has traveled a long and fascinating journey, one that reflects both the power of art and the complexities of cultural heritage. Despite its missing arms, or perhaps because of them, the Venus de Milo remains a masterpiece that invites endless interpretation and admiration. Its beauty, elegance, and sense of mystery continue to captivate audiences, making it one of the most beloved and iconic sculptures in the history of art. Today, the Venus de Milo stands not only as a testament to the skill of ancient Greek sculptors but also as a symbol of the enduring appeal of classical art, a reminder that beauty, even in its most incomplete form, can transcend time and place to inspire generations of viewers.

Chapter 14: The Largest Paintings in the Louvre

The Louvre Museum is home to some of the most iconic and vast collections of art in the world, including monumental paintings that capture the grand scale and dramatic power of historical, religious, and mythological events. While the museum is often celebrated for its intimate masterpieces like the "Mona Lisa" or the "Venus de Milo," the largest paintings in the Louvre offer an equally compelling experience, immersing visitors in expansive scenes filled with intricate details and sweeping narratives. These enormous canvases, some of which stretch nearly the length of entire walls, are impressive not only for their size but also for their masterful composition, vivid storytelling, and historical significance. Understanding these large-scale works requires delving into their subject matter, the artists who created them, and the historical contexts in which they were painted.

One of the largest and most famous paintings in the Louvre is *"The Coronation of Napoleon"* by Jacques-Louis David, a monumental work that measures an astonishing 6.21 meters (20.37 feet) tall and 9.79 meters (32.1 feet) wide. Painted between 1805 and 1807, this massive canvas depicts the momentous event of Napoleon Bonaparte's coronation as Emperor of the French, which took place in the Notre-Dame Cathedral in Paris in 1804. David, a leading figure of the Neoclassical movement and Napoleon's official court painter, was commissioned to create this grandiose painting as a way of immortalizing the splendor and authority of Napoleon's rule.

The sheer scale of the painting allows David to include a vast array of figures, each carefully rendered to convey the importance of the event. At the center of the composition is Napoleon, standing tall and regal as he crowns his wife, Josephine, in a gesture of self-coronation. This moment, in which Napoleon crowns himself rather than allowing the Pope to perform the ceremony, symbolized his assertion of supreme power and independence from the Church. Surrounding Napoleon and Josephine are numerous dignitaries, clergy, and members of the imperial family, all of whom are depicted with meticulous attention to detail. The grandeur of the cathedral's interior, with its soaring arches and flickering candlelight, further adds to the sense of awe and ceremony.

David's *"The Coronation of Napoleon"* is not only a masterpiece of Neoclassical art but also a complex political statement. By choosing to highlight Napoleon's self-coronation, David reinforced the narrative of Napoleon as a self-made ruler who rose to power through his own merits and abilities. At the same time, the painting celebrates the splendor and authority of the new French Empire, with every element carefully designed to evoke a sense of grandeur and legitimacy. The size of the canvas allows for an immersive experience, drawing viewers into the ceremony and encouraging them to reflect on the historical significance of the event. Today, *"The Coronation of Napoleon"* remains one of the Louvre's most popular attractions, with visitors standing in awe of its monumental scale and exquisite detail.

Another of the Louvre's largest and most important paintings is *"The Wedding Feast at Cana"* by Paolo Veronese, which measures an astounding 6.77 meters (22.2 feet) tall and 9.94 meters (32.6 feet) wide, making it the largest painting in the museum. This massive canvas was completed in 1563 by the Venetian master and was originally commissioned for the refectory of the Benedictine Monastery of San Giorgio Maggiore in Venice. The painting depicts the biblical story of the Wedding at Cana, in which Christ performed the miracle of turning water into wine, his first recorded miracle in the New Testament.

Veronese's *"The Wedding Feast at Cana"* is a dazzling display of color, light, and movement, filled with hundreds of figures that populate the grand banquet scene. The painting is divided into two main levels: the lower half, where the wedding feast is taking place, and the upper half, where the architecture and sky create a majestic backdrop. At the center of the composition is Christ, seated calmly at the table, surrounded by the wedding guests, musicians, and servants. The figures are dressed in opulent clothing, reflecting the sumptuousness and extravagance of Renaissance Venice. The artist's use of perspective and spatial arrangement draws the viewer's eye toward Christ, emphasizing his role in the miracle while simultaneously showcasing the lavishness of the feast.

What makes *"The Wedding Feast at Cana"* truly remarkable is its ability to capture both the spiritual and the earthly aspects of the scene. While the focus of the painting is on the miracle, Veronese fills the composition with lively details of daily life, from the bustling servants to the musicians tuning their instruments. The grand architecture, with its towering columns and intricate balustrades, enhances the sense of magnificence, turning the biblical story into a celebration of human life and divine intervention. The painting's enormous size amplifies its impact, allowing viewers to feel as though they are part of the feast, witnessing the miracle firsthand. Today, *"The Wedding Feast at Cana"* stands opposite Leonardo da Vinci's *"Mona Lisa"* in the Louvre, creating a striking contrast between the intimate, contemplative gaze of the small portrait and the dynamic, sprawling energy of Veronese's masterpiece.

Another monumental work in the Louvre's collection is *"The Raft of the Medusa"* by Théodore Géricault, which measures 4.91 meters (16.1 feet) tall and 7.16 meters (23.5 feet) wide. Painted between 1818 and 1819, this powerful painting depicts the aftermath of a tragic shipwreck that occurred in 1816, when the French frigate *Medusa* ran aground off the coast of Senegal. Due to a lack of lifeboats, 147 people were left stranded on a makeshift raft, and after days of starvation, dehydration, and cannibalism, only 15 survivors were rescued.

Géricault's painting captures the desperate moment when the survivors first spot a ship on the horizon, their last hope for salvation.

"The Raft of the Medusa" is a masterpiece of Romanticism, a movement that emphasized emotion, individual experience, and the sublime power of nature. Géricault's use of dramatic lighting, bold contrasts, and intense expressions heightens the emotional impact of the scene. The composition is structured around the diagonal sweep of the raft, with the bodies of the survivors piled in chaotic disorder. Some figures are already dead, their limp forms draped over the edge of the raft, while others stretch upward in a final act of hope and desperation. The stark contrast between the light breaking through the stormy clouds and the dark, turbulent sea creates a sense of impending doom and tenuous hope.

What makes *"The Raft of the Medusa"* particularly compelling is its raw, unflinching portrayal of human suffering and survival. Géricault conducted extensive research for the painting, interviewing survivors, visiting morgues to study dead bodies, and even constructing a life-size model of the raft in his studio to ensure the accuracy of the scene. The painting is not only a depiction of a historical event but also a powerful commentary on human endurance in the face of tragedy and the incompetence of the French government, whose mishandling of the shipwreck scandalized the public. The immense size of the canvas magnifies the horror and drama of the scene, making it impossible for viewers to ignore the suffering and struggle of the survivors. The painting's influence on later art, especially within the Romantic and Realist movements, is profound, and it remains one of the Louvre's most visited and discussed works.

"The Battle of San Romano" by Paolo Uccello is another large painting in the Louvre's collection, though it is part of a triptych, with the other two panels housed in different museums. The panel in the Louvre measures 1.82 meters (6 feet) tall and 3.2 meters (10.5 feet) wide. This Renaissance masterpiece depicts the Florentine army's

victory over the Sienese forces at the Battle of San Romano in 1432. Uccello's painting is known for its use of perspective and foreshortening, techniques that were revolutionary in the early Renaissance and which give the scene a sense of depth and movement. The battlefield is filled with knights on horseback, armed with lances and swords, their armor gleaming in the sunlight. Uccello's attention to detail and geometric composition creates a stylized, almost abstract effect, turning the chaos of battle into a carefully orchestrated dance of forms and lines.

While smaller than some of the other monumental works in the Louvre, *"The Battle of San Romano"* stands out for its historical importance and its innovative use of perspective. Uccello's fascination with geometry and his desire to depict three-dimensional space on a two-dimensional surface marked a turning point in the history of art, influencing generations of artists who sought to master the illusion of depth. The painting's scale allows Uccello to depict the complexity of the battle in all its detail, from the charging horses to the fallen soldiers, creating a dynamic and immersive experience for the viewer.

In addition to these famous examples, the Louvre houses many other large-scale paintings, each offering a unique window into the past and the artistic movements that shaped their creation. From the dramatic, emotionally charged works of the Romantic era to the meticulously detailed compositions of the Renaissance, these monumental paintings demonstrate the power of art to convey the grand narratives of history, myth, and human experience. The size of these works is not merely a technical feat but a testament to the ambition and skill of the artists who created them, as well as the importance of the subjects they depict.

The largest paintings in the Louvre offer a different kind of encounter with art than smaller, more intimate works. Their size demands attention, drawing viewers in and surrounding them with the world of the painting. These works often depict grand historical or religious events, and their scale allows the artist to explore the complexity of these scenes in rich detail. The viewer is not just a passive observer but is invited to engage with the painting on a deeper level, contemplating the emotions, actions, and significance of the figures and events portrayed.

Ultimately, the largest paintings in the Louvre are masterpieces not only of technical skill and artistic vision but also of storytelling and historical memory. They capture moments of triumph, tragedy, and transformation, offering viewers a chance to step back in time and witness the grandeur of human history as interpreted by some of the greatest artists of all time. These monumental works stand as enduring testaments to the power of art to communicate across centuries, transcending their immense size to connect with viewers on a deeply personal and emotional level. As visitors to the Louvre continue to be captivated by these towering masterpieces, the legacy of these artists and their works remains as vital and powerful as ever.

Chapter 15: How Art is Preserved at the Louvre

The preservation of art at the Louvre is a fascinating and complex process that combines centuries-old traditions with the latest technological advances. As one of the largest and most important museums in the world, the Louvre is home to a staggering collection of over 380,000 works of art, ranging from ancient sculptures to Renaissance masterpieces, Islamic art, and modern pieces. The museum's responsibility is immense, as it not only displays these priceless objects but also ensures that they are preserved for future generations. This task requires a multidisciplinary approach, involving art conservators, curators, scientists, engineers, and many other specialists who work behind the scenes to protect the museum's treasures from the ravages of time, environmental factors, and even potential threats like theft or natural disasters.

One of the most important aspects of preserving art at the Louvre is the control of environmental conditions. Paintings, sculptures, and other types of artwork are highly sensitive to changes in temperature, humidity, light, and pollutants, all of which can cause irreversible damage if not properly regulated. For example, fluctuations in temperature can cause the materials used in paintings—such as canvas, wood, or paint—to expand and contract, leading to cracks, warping, or other forms of deterioration. Similarly, excessive humidity can promote the growth of mold and mildew, while too little humidity can cause materials to dry out and become brittle. To prevent these issues, the Louvre uses advanced climate control systems that carefully regulate the temperature and humidity in each gallery, ensuring that the conditions are optimal for preserving the artworks on display.

The Louvre's conservators pay special attention to the levels of light that illuminate the artworks, as exposure to ultraviolet (UV) and infrared light can fade colors and weaken materials over time. Natural light, in particular, can be harmful to paintings, textiles, and other delicate objects, which is why many of the museum's galleries are equipped with filters that block out harmful UV rays. In some cases, windows are covered or shaded to minimize direct sunlight, while artificial lighting is carefully calibrated to provide enough illumination for visitors to see the art without causing damage. For especially sensitive works, like illuminated manuscripts or textiles, the amount of time they are exposed to light is often limited, with the objects rotated in and out of storage to reduce their exposure to potentially harmful lighting conditions.

In addition to controlling environmental factors, the Louvre employs a team of highly skilled conservators who specialize in the restoration and conservation of artworks. These professionals are trained in a wide range of techniques that allow them to repair damaged works of art, stabilize fragile objects, and prevent further deterioration. Conservation work can be extremely delicate, as it often involves working with ancient or fragile materials that require careful handling and precise interventions. For instance, when restoring a painting, conservators may use microscopic tools to remove layers of dirt or old varnish that have accumulated over centuries, revealing the original colors and details of the artwork. In some cases, they may also need to repair tears in the canvas or cracks in the paint, using materials that are carefully chosen to match the original and to ensure the longevity of the restoration.

One famous example of art conservation at the Louvre is the restoration of Leonardo da Vinci's *Mona Lisa*. Over the centuries, this iconic painting has undergone several restorations to address issues such as discoloration, cracks in the paint, and damage from past cleaning efforts. The *Mona Lisa* is now housed in a specially designed, climate-controlled case that protects it from environmental fluctuations, dust, and even potential vandalism. The case is made of bulletproof glass, which not only safeguards the painting from physical damage but also reduces the exposure to harmful light. Additionally, the air inside the case is carefully regulated to maintain a stable temperature and humidity, ensuring that the painting remains in optimal condition for future generations to enjoy.

Conserving sculptures presents a different set of challenges, as these three-dimensional objects are often made from a wide range of materials, including marble, bronze, wood, and ceramics. Each material requires a unique approach to conservation, as they respond differently to environmental factors and age in different ways. For example, bronze sculptures can develop a greenish patina over time due to oxidation, which may be desirable in some cases (as it can add historical character) but damaging in others. Conservators must carefully assess each sculpture to determine the best course of action, whether it's cleaning the surface, repairing cracks or breaks, or stabilizing the material to prevent further deterioration.

One particularly notable sculpture in the Louvre's collection that has undergone extensive conservation work is the *Winged Victory of Samothrace*, an ancient Greek masterpiece that dates back to the 2nd century BCE. Discovered in pieces on the island of Samothrace in the 19th century, the statue was painstakingly reassembled and restored over the course of several decades. More recently, in 2013-2014, the *Winged Victory* underwent another major restoration, during which conservators carefully cleaned the surface of the marble, removed old restorations that had discolored over time, and stabilized the statue to ensure its continued preservation. The process was carried out with the utmost care, using non-invasive techniques that preserved the integrity of the original material while enhancing the statue's appearance for modern viewers.

Another critical aspect of art preservation at the Louvre is preventive conservation, which focuses on identifying and mitigating potential risks before they cause damage. Preventive conservation involves a wide range of activities, from monitoring environmental conditions and controlling pests to ensuring that artworks are properly handled, stored, and displayed. For example, when transporting artworks within the museum or loaning them to other institutions for exhibitions, the Louvre uses specially designed crates and packaging materials that protect the objects from physical shocks, vibrations, and fluctuations in temperature and humidity. Art handlers are trained in best practices for moving fragile objects, ensuring that they are transported safely and without risk of damage.

Preventive conservation also extends to the museum's storage facilities, where a large portion of the collection is kept when not on display. The Louvre has state-of-the-art storage areas that are designed to maintain optimal environmental conditions for preserving the artworks. Each object is carefully cataloged and stored in a manner that minimizes the risk of damage, whether it's by placing paintings in specially designed racks, housing sculptures in padded crates, or storing fragile textiles in climate-controlled rooms. These storage areas are regularly monitored to ensure that the environmental conditions remain stable, and conservators conduct periodic inspections of the collection to identify any potential issues that may require intervention.

Technology plays an increasingly important role in art preservation at the Louvre. Advances in scientific research have allowed conservators to gain a deeper understanding of the materials and techniques used by artists throughout history, which in turn informs the methods used to conserve and restore works of art. For example, X-ray fluorescence (XRF) and infrared reflectography are commonly used to examine paintings beneath the surface layers of paint, revealing hidden details, underdrawings, and previous restorations. This information helps conservators make more informed decisions about how to approach the restoration process, ensuring that their interventions are as accurate and respectful of the original work as possible.

One cutting-edge technology that has revolutionized art conservation is 3D scanning, which allows conservators to create highly detailed digital models of sculptures and other three-dimensional objects. These scans provide a precise record of an object's current condition, which can be used to monitor changes over time and to plan restoration work. In some cases, 3D printing technology is also used to create replicas of missing or damaged parts of sculptures, allowing conservators to restore the original appearance of the work without altering the original material. This is particularly useful for ancient statues and other archaeological artifacts that have been damaged or eroded over time.

The Louvre's commitment to preserving art also extends beyond the museum's walls. As a leading cultural institution, the Louvre plays an active role in the global effort to preserve cultural heritage, often collaborating with other museums, universities, and research institutions on conservation projects. The museum provides training and expertise to institutions around the world, helping to promote best practices in art conservation and to protect vulnerable collections from threats such as environmental degradation, conflict, and neglect. The Louvre's involvement in international conservation efforts highlights the importance of preserving cultural heritage not just for the museum's visitors but for humanity as a whole.

In recent years, the threat of climate change has added new challenges to the preservation of art at the Louvre. Rising temperatures, increased humidity, and more frequent extreme weather events all pose risks to the museum's collection, particularly for works that are sensitive to environmental fluctuations. In response, the Louvre has implemented a range of sustainability initiatives aimed at reducing the museum's carbon footprint and improving the resilience of its infrastructure. For example, the museum has installed energy-efficient climate control systems, improved insulation in its galleries and storage areas, and developed strategies for protecting the collection from potential flooding, especially given the Louvre's location near the Seine River.

One of the Louvre's most ambitious recent projects is the construction of a new conservation center in Liévin, near Lens, France. This facility, which opened in 2019, is designed to house and protect much of the museum's collection in a state-of-the-art environment, with optimal conditions for preserving art. The center features advanced climate control systems, secure storage facilities, and dedicated spaces for conservation research and restoration work. By relocating a significant portion of the collection to this new facility, the Louvre is better equipped to protect its treasures from the risks posed by both environmental factors and overcrowding in its main building in Paris.

In conclusion, the preservation of art at the Louvre is a highly sophisticated process that requires a combination of scientific knowledge, technical expertise, and a deep respect for the artistic and cultural significance of the works in the museum's collection. Through careful monitoring of environmental conditions, meticulous conservation work, and the use of cutting-edge technology, the Louvre ensures that its priceless treasures remain safe and accessible for future generations. At the same time, the museum continues to play a leading role in the global effort to protect cultural heritage, recognizing that the preservation of art is not just about safeguarding objects but about preserving the history, identity, and creativity of humanity itself.

Chapter 16: The Louvre's Hidden Courtyards

The Louvre, known for its vast collection of priceless art and rich historical significance, also hides a fascinating architectural element that many visitors may overlook: its hidden courtyards. These courtyards, tucked away within the sprawling complex of the Louvre, are serene, often tranquil spaces, serving as a stark contrast to the bustling galleries filled with tourists and art enthusiasts. They hold within them layers of history, architecture, and aesthetic beauty that contribute to the Louvre's charm as more than just a repository of art. Exploring these secluded spaces opens up an entirely different facet of the museum—one that speaks to its evolution from a medieval fortress to a royal palace, and eventually, the world-renowned museum it is today. The courtyards are an integral part of the Louvre's transformation over the centuries, reflecting both the architectural and cultural shifts that shaped the building and its role in French history.

The Louvre began as a medieval fortress built by King Philippe Auguste in the late 12th century, designed to defend Paris from invasion. The original fortress included an enclosed courtyard, or "cour carrée" (square courtyard), which was surrounded by tall defensive walls and towers. Over time, as the Louvre was expanded and transformed into a royal residence, this early courtyard became the foundation upon which the palace's courtyards would evolve. The transition from fortress to palace saw the construction of additional wings and courtyards, each reflecting the architectural styles of the era and the tastes of the monarchs who commissioned them.

One of the most significant transformations of the Louvre's courtyards occurred during the Renaissance under King François I, who sought to modernize the medieval fortress into a grand palace that reflected the artistic and intellectual achievements of his time. François

I invited Italian architects and artists, including Leonardo da Vinci, to France, and their influence is evident in the Louvre's architectural evolution. The medieval courtyard was transformed into the Cour Carrée, a grand and harmonious space that became the centerpiece of the Louvre's Renaissance transformation. The Cour Carrée, with its classical proportions and elegant arches, embodies the ideals of Renaissance architecture, blending symmetry, balance, and beauty in a way that stands in contrast to the fortress-like structures that had previously defined the Louvre.

The Cour Carrée, however, is just one of several courtyards within the Louvre, each with its own unique history and character. As the Louvre continued to expand under subsequent monarchs, new wings were added, creating additional courtyards that reflected the changing tastes and architectural styles of the time. For instance, the Cour Napoleon, named after Napoleon Bonaparte, who had a profound influence on the Louvre during his reign, is one of the museum's most famous open spaces today. Dominated by I. M. Pei's modern glass pyramid, the Cour Napoleon serves as the main entrance to the museum, blending contemporary design with the historic grandeur of the surrounding palace.

Before the installation of the pyramid in 1989, however, the Cour Napoleon was a much more secluded and less prominent space. In the centuries before Pei's pyramid was erected, the courtyard had served various practical functions, including as a military parade ground during the reign of Louis XIV. It wasn't until the late 20th century, with the expansion of the museum and the introduction of the Grand Louvre project, that the Cour Napoleon became the focal point it is today, linking the Louvre's past with its modern identity as an international center for art and culture.

Another hidden courtyard within the Louvre complex is the Cour Marly, which was originally an outdoor courtyard but has since been enclosed by a glass roof to create the Marly Courtyard Sculpture

Garden. The Cour Marly takes its name from Château de Marly, a royal residence built for Louis XIV near Versailles. The sculptures displayed in this courtyard are magnificent examples of 17th- and 18th-century French statuary, many of which originally adorned the gardens of Marly. The Louvre has transformed the courtyard into an elegant space where visitors can admire these statues in a serene, light-filled environment, surrounded by the classical architecture of the Louvre. The glass ceiling allows natural light to pour into the space, creating a beautiful interplay of light and shadow that changes throughout the day, making the sculptures appear almost alive as the lighting shifts. The Cour Marly is a stunning example of how the Louvre has repurposed its courtyards over time, adapting them to house specific collections and enhancing the visitor experience by creating intimate, immersive environments for viewing art.

Similarly, the Cour Puget, located near the Cour Marly, is another hidden gem within the Louvre that has been transformed into a sculpture garden. Named after the French Baroque sculptor Pierre Puget, this courtyard features a collection of large-scale sculptures, many of which were originally commissioned for the gardens of Versailles and other royal estates. Like the Cour Marly, the Cour Puget has been enclosed by a glass roof, allowing for the preservation of the sculptures while creating a beautiful, light-filled space that feels both intimate and grand. The glass roof of the Cour Puget, designed by architect Ieoh Ming Pei as part of the Grand Louvre renovation project, is a masterpiece of modern engineering, seamlessly integrating contemporary design with the historical architecture of the Louvre. Visitors to the Cour Puget can wander among the statues, taking in their dynamic forms and intricate details while enjoying the peaceful, almost meditative atmosphere of the courtyard.

These hidden courtyards, such as the Cour Marly and Cour Puget, provide a stark contrast to the crowded galleries of the Louvre, offering visitors a quiet retreat where they can appreciate the art in a more contemplative setting. The courtyards' transformation into enclosed sculpture gardens is a testament to the Louvre's ability to adapt its spaces to suit the changing needs of the museum and its visitors, while also preserving the historical integrity of the building.

The history of the Louvre's courtyards is closely tied to the evolution of the museum itself, reflecting the changing architectural styles, political shifts, and cultural developments that have shaped the institution over the centuries. During the reign of Louis XIV, the Louvre underwent significant expansion, with the addition of new wings and courtyards that reflected the opulence and grandeur of the Sun King's court. The Cour du Carrousel, for example, was created as part of the expansion of the Louvre under Louis XIV, and it originally served as a grand space for royal processions and ceremonies. The name "Carrousel" refers to a lavish equestrian display held in 1662 to celebrate the birth of Louis XIV's son, the Dauphin. Today, the Cour du Carrousel is one of the Louvre's largest courtyards, bordered by the Arc de Triomphe du Carrousel, a triumphal arch built by Napoleon to commemorate his military victories. The courtyard's vast expanse and its historical significance make it a key part of the Louvre's architectural landscape, offering visitors a sense of the royal pomp and ceremony that once characterized the palace.

Despite their beauty and historical significance, the Louvre's courtyards have not always been accessible to the public. For much of the museum's history, these spaces were reserved for the exclusive use of the royal family and their court, serving as private gardens, ceremonial spaces, and even military training grounds. It wasn't until the Louvre was transformed into a public museum after the French Revolution that these courtyards became accessible to ordinary citizens. The opening of the Louvre to the public in 1793 marked a radical shift in the function of the building, as it was no longer a symbol of royal power but a space for the celebration of art and culture. The courtyards, once the domain of kings and nobles, became part of the public's experience of the Louvre, offering new opportunities for exploration and discovery.

Today, these hidden courtyards continue to play an important role in the life of the Louvre. They serve not only as spaces for displaying art but also as places of rest and reflection for visitors. After navigating the museum's vast galleries, filled with world-renowned masterpieces, the courtyards offer a peaceful respite where visitors can take a moment to relax and absorb the beauty around them. Whether strolling through the sculpture gardens of the Cour Marly and Cour Puget, admiring the Renaissance architecture of the Cour Carrée, or marveling at the glass pyramid in the Cour Napoleon, visitors to the Louvre can experience the museum in a more intimate and personal way by exploring these often-overlooked spaces.

The courtyards also reflect the Louvre's ongoing commitment to preserving and enhancing its historic architecture while integrating modern design elements. The Grand Louvre project, which began in the 1980s, was a pivotal moment in the museum's history, as it sought to modernize the Louvre while respecting its architectural heritage. The project included the renovation of several courtyards, the addition of the glass pyramids, and the creation of new exhibition spaces that have made the museum more accessible to the millions of visitors who pass through its doors each year. The careful balance between preserving the past and embracing the future is evident in the Louvre's courtyards, where the old and the new coexist in harmony, offering visitors a glimpse into the rich history of the museum while providing modern amenities and experiences.

In conclusion, the Louvre's hidden courtyards are an integral part of the museum's architecture and history, offering visitors a unique perspective on the evolution of one of the world's greatest cultural institutions. These secluded spaces, with their blend of historical grandeur and contemporary design, provide a quiet refuge from the bustling galleries and an opportunity to experience the museum in a more personal and reflective way. From the Renaissance beauty of the Cour Carrée to the modern sculpture gardens of the Cour Marly and Cour Puget, the Louvre's courtyards reveal the layers of history that have shaped the museum and continue to influence its role as a global center for art and culture.

Chapter 17: Visiting the Louvre at Night

Visiting the Louvre at night is a magical and unique experience that transforms one of the world's most famous museums into an enchanting realm of art, history, and architecture bathed in soft, atmospheric lighting. The Louvre by day is an awe-inspiring destination, filled with bustling crowds, the sound of footsteps echoing through its grand halls, and the hum of excited voices discussing its treasures. By night, however, the Louvre takes on a completely different character. The vastness of its galleries, the monumental architecture, and the sense of history that pervades the building become even more pronounced, creating a surreal and almost dreamlike experience for those lucky enough to explore its halls after sunset. The artworks, illuminated by carefully designed lighting, appear more vivid and captivating, while the quieter, more intimate atmosphere allows for deeper contemplation and appreciation of the masterpieces on display.

One of the most immediate differences when visiting the Louvre at night is the reduced crowd size. During the day, the museum is typically filled with visitors from around the world, making it one of the busiest cultural destinations on the planet. While this adds to the energy and excitement of the experience, it can also make it difficult to fully appreciate some of the more famous works, like the *Mona Lisa*, *Venus de Milo*, or *Winged Victory of Samothrace*, which are often surrounded by large groups of people. At night, however, the number of visitors drops significantly, allowing for a more leisurely and peaceful exploration of the museum. This means that you can spend more time in front of your favorite artworks without feeling rushed, taking in every detail and nuance that might be missed in the daytime crowds. The quieter galleries create an atmosphere of solitude and reverence, giving visitors the sense that they have the museum almost to themselves.

The Louvre's iconic glass pyramid, which serves as the main entrance to the museum, is another element that takes on a new dimension at night. Designed by architect I. M. Pei and completed in 1989, the pyramid is made of glass and metal, standing in stark contrast to the surrounding classical architecture of the Louvre Palace. During the day, the pyramid reflects the sunlight and the vibrant energy of Paris, but at night, it becomes a beacon of light, glowing softly against the dark sky. The pyramid and its smaller counterparts, which are part of the museum's courtyard, are illuminated from within, creating a mesmerizing spectacle that draws visitors into the museum. The juxtaposition of the modern pyramid with the centuries-old Louvre buildings, all bathed in warm, golden light, is a sight to behold and one of the most photogenic scenes in Paris. Many visitors to the Louvre at night make a point of lingering outside the museum just to take in this stunning visual, where history and modernity meet in a breathtaking way.

The experience of walking through the Louvre's galleries at night is heightened by the way the artworks are illuminated. The museum employs carefully designed lighting systems that accentuate the details of each piece, casting shadows that bring out the textures and contours of sculptures and paintings. In some cases, the lighting helps to reveal details that might not be as noticeable during the day, such as the brushstrokes on a painting or the fine chiseling of a marble statue. For visitors who are particularly interested in art appreciation, this lighting adds an extra layer of depth to the experience, allowing for a more immersive and focused engagement with the works. The Louvre's vast collection is so extensive that it can be overwhelming to take it all in during the day, but at night, when the pace slows down, there is more time to absorb and reflect on each masterpiece in a deeper and more personal way.

Another benefit of visiting the Louvre at night is the ability to experience the museum's impressive architecture under different lighting conditions. The Louvre Palace, with its Renaissance and Baroque facades, is one of the most architecturally significant buildings in Paris. By day, the palace is a majestic symbol of French history and culture, but at night, the play of light and shadow across its stone walls, columns, and statues creates an even more dramatic effect. The intricate details of the palace's exterior, including its carvings, sculptures, and decorative elements, become more pronounced in the low light, giving visitors a new perspective on the building's beauty. Inside the museum, the grandeur of the Louvre's interiors is equally enhanced by the evening lighting. The long, marble corridors, the grand staircases, and the opulent halls feel even more stately and awe-inspiring when illuminated at night, evoking a sense of mystery and timelessness.

One of the most famous galleries to visit at night is the Denon Wing, which houses some of the museum's most iconic works, including Leonardo da Vinci's *Mona Lisa* and Théodore Géricault's *The Raft of the Medusa*. The dim lighting in this wing, combined with the reduced crowds, allows for a more intimate viewing experience of these masterpieces. Visitors can stand quietly in front of the *Mona Lisa*, examining the painting's fine details without the distraction of other tourists jostling for position. The enigmatic smile of Leonardo's most famous subject seems to take on an even greater mystery when viewed in the soft glow of the gallery's lights. Meanwhile, Géricault's *The Raft of the Medusa*, with its dramatic depiction of shipwrecked survivors clinging to life, feels even more intense and emotional when viewed in the hushed, semi-darkness of the evening hours.

Sculpture lovers will also find the Louvre at night to be a particularly rewarding experience. The museum's many sculpture galleries, such as the Cour Marly and the Cour Puget, are stunning at night, with the sculptures dramatically lit to highlight their forms and details. The enclosed courtyards, with their glass roofs and expansive open spaces, create an almost ethereal atmosphere, as the statues seem to come alive in the shifting light. The combination of natural and artificial lighting in these spaces creates a play of shadows that brings out the dynamism of the sculptures, making them appear even more lifelike. Whether it's the heroic figures of ancient Greece and Rome, the delicate beauty of Renaissance works, or the powerful forms of 18th- and 19th-century French sculptures, the Louvre's sculpture collection takes on a whole new dimension when viewed at night.

For visitors interested in exploring the Louvre's vast collection of ancient art, a nighttime visit offers a special opportunity to experience the museum's galleries of Egyptian, Greek, Roman, and Near Eastern antiquities in a more reflective and meditative setting. The artifacts in these galleries, which include everything from intricately carved sarcophagi to colossal statues of pharaohs, feel even more mysterious and awe-inspiring when viewed in the low light of the evening. The sense of history in these galleries is palpable, as visitors walk among the remnants of ancient civilizations, illuminated by the soft glow of carefully positioned lights that enhance the beauty and significance of each piece.

Another highlight of visiting the Louvre at night is the opportunity to see special exhibitions in a more relaxed environment. The museum frequently hosts temporary exhibitions that focus on specific artists, periods, or themes, and these exhibitions are often popular and crowded during the day. However, at night, visitors have more space and time to explore these exhibitions at their leisure, making it easier to absorb the information and engage with the artworks on a deeper level. Whether it's a retrospective of a major artist, a thematic exploration of a particular period in art history, or an exhibition focused on a specific medium, visiting these temporary shows at night allows for a more focused and enjoyable experience.

The Louvre's evening hours also offer a chance to experience some of the museum's lesser-known and quieter galleries, which are often overlooked during the day when visitors tend to focus on the most famous works. Exploring these hidden gems at night can be a rewarding experience, as many of these galleries contain incredible works of art that deserve just as much attention as the Louvre's more famous pieces. For example, the museum's collection of Islamic art, housed in the Department of Islamic Arts, is a breathtaking showcase of decorative arts, textiles, ceramics, and metalwork from across the Islamic world. The collection is displayed in a modern, purpose-built gallery that is beautifully lit at night, allowing visitors to fully appreciate the intricate designs and craftsmanship of these works.

The Louvre's nighttime experience extends beyond the galleries, as the museum often hosts special events and activities during its evening hours. These can include guided tours, lectures, and performances, all designed to offer visitors a deeper understanding of the museum's collection and history. Nighttime tours of the Louvre are particularly popular, as they provide a more intimate and focused exploration of specific works or themes within the museum. Led by knowledgeable guides, these tours offer insights into the stories behind the artworks, the artists who created them, and the historical context in which they were made. For those interested in a more interactive experience, the Louvre's evening programming also sometimes includes live performances, such as concerts or theater productions, which take place in some of the museum's grand halls or courtyards, adding another layer of cultural engagement to the visit.

As visitors make their way through the Louvre at night, they are often struck by the sense of history and timelessness that pervades the museum. The Louvre has been a central part of French history for over 800 years, evolving from a medieval fortress to a royal palace, and finally to one of the world's greatest museums. Walking through its galleries at night, with the shadows of centuries past lingering in the air, visitors can feel the weight of this history in a profound way. The Louvre's walls have witnessed the rise and fall of kings, the turmoil of revolutions, and the birth of artistic movements that have shaped the world. To visit the Louvre at night is to step into this history, to be surrounded by the echoes of the past while engaging with the timeless beauty of art.

In conclusion, visiting the Louvre at night is an unforgettable experience that offers a new and captivating perspective on one of the world's greatest cultural institutions. From the reduced crowds and peaceful atmosphere to the beautifully illuminated artworks and architecture, the Louvre takes on a magical quality after dark. Whether you are a seasoned art lover or a first-time visitor, exploring the museum at night allows for a deeper and more personal connection with its masterpieces, offering moments of quiet reflection and awe. The experience of seeing the Louvre's treasures under the soft glow of evening light, combined with the museum's rich history and architectural beauty, makes a nighttime visit to the Louvre a truly special and unique experience.

Chapter 18: The Louvre's Role in World War II

The Louvre's role during World War II is a compelling chapter in the museum's long history, filled with dramatic events, daring efforts to protect art, and the broader significance of the museum as a cultural symbol during one of the darkest periods in global history. The story of the Louvre during the war is marked by both tragedy and heroism, as curators, art historians, and everyday citizens worked tirelessly to safeguard the museum's vast collection from the threat of Nazi looting, destruction, and the ravages of war. This period also highlights the broader struggle to protect cultural heritage in times of conflict, emphasizing the value of art and history as essential elements of a nation's identity and humanity's shared heritage.

When World War II erupted in 1939, the Louvre was one of the most important cultural institutions in the world. Its vast collection, including masterpieces like the *Mona Lisa, Venus de Milo,* and *Winged Victory of Samothrace,* was not only a testament to human creativity but also a symbol of French national pride. As the Nazi regime expanded across Europe, looting art became a key part of its strategy. The Nazis viewed art as both a trophy of war and a tool for propaganda. Adolf Hitler, in particular, was obsessed with art, having been an aspiring painter in his youth, and sought to amass the greatest art collection in the world to fill the Führermuseum he planned to build in Linz, Austria. At the same time, Nazi leaders like Hermann Göring saw art as a valuable commodity, hoarding countless works for their personal collections. With this in mind, the directors and curators of the Louvre, led by Jacques Jaujard, the museum's director, recognized the imminent danger and began to take steps to protect the museum's priceless treasures long before Paris fell to the Nazis.

In late 1939, as the threat of German invasion grew more palpable, Jaujard orchestrated a massive and highly secretive evacuation of the Louvre's most valuable works of art. Over the course of several months, thousands of paintings, sculptures, and artifacts were carefully packed and transported out of Paris to various locations across the French countryside. This evacuation was an extraordinary logistical feat, involving not only the museum's staff but also local volunteers, truck drivers, and railway workers. Jaujard's plan involved moving the artworks to a network of châteaux, abbeys, and private estates, where they would be hidden from the Nazis. The aim was to scatter the collection across as many locations as possible, reducing the risk that a single bombing raid or seizure by Nazi forces could result in the loss of the entire collection.

The evacuation process was fraught with challenges. Many of the artworks were extremely fragile and required special handling, while others were too large to be easily transported. The *Mona Lisa*, arguably the most famous painting in the Louvre's collection, was a particular concern. The painting had already been targeted by thieves in the past, and its immense cultural significance made it a prime target for Nazi looters. In an operation that resembled a military maneuver, the *Mona Lisa* was transported in a custom-made, airtight container to the Château de Chambord, one of the most secure locations used during the evacuation. The *Venus de Milo* and *Winged Victory of Samothrace*, both monumental sculptures, were also packed and transported with extreme care. Despite the challenges, by the time the Nazis entered Paris in June 1940, most of the Louvre's most valuable pieces had been successfully evacuated, leaving behind only a fraction of the museum's collection.

Once the Nazis occupied Paris, the Louvre itself fell under the control of the German military. While many of the most valuable works had been removed, the museum still housed thousands of lesser-known but still important pieces of art. The Nazis, under the direction of Alfred Rosenberg's ERR (Einsatzstab Reichsleiter Rosenberg), a task force dedicated to looting cultural property, began systematically cataloging and looting the remaining works in the Louvre and other French museums. The ERR was responsible for seizing thousands of works of art from Jewish families, galleries, and collectors, which they then shipped back to Germany. Although the Louvre's evacuated works were largely safe from the Nazis, the museum itself became a staging ground for the looting and redistribution of French art and cultural property.

Jacques Jaujard, however, remained in Paris throughout the occupation, working behind the scenes to protect French cultural heritage. He maintained contact with the Resistance and was instrumental in thwarting several attempts by the Nazis to locate the evacuated artworks. Jaujard also played a key role in preserving the integrity of the Louvre's collection by keeping detailed records of the evacuated works, ensuring that they could be returned to the museum once the war ended. His actions were part of a broader network of French Resistance efforts to protect cultural heritage, including the work of art historians, curators, and everyday citizens who risked their lives to safeguard France's artistic legacy.

Meanwhile, as the war progressed, the châteaux and estates where the Louvre's evacuated works were hidden faced increasing danger. The German military began to take control of these properties, using them as headquarters or storage depots. In some cases, the art was at risk of being discovered by German officers who were unaware of its presence. The caretakers and curators who had accompanied the artworks to these locations often lived in constant fear of discovery, knowing that if the Nazis found the art, it would be seized or destroyed. In one instance, the *Mona Lisa* was nearly discovered when German officers commandeered the Château de Chambord, but the caretakers managed to keep its location a secret.

As the tide of the war began to turn in favor of the Allies, the Nazis became increasingly desperate to hold on to the art they had looted. In 1944, as Allied forces advanced into France, Nazi leaders ordered the systematic removal of looted art from France to Germany. The ERR and other Nazi agencies scrambled to transport as many artworks as possible before the Allies arrived. However, French Resistance fighters and Allied forces, including the famous Monuments Men, a group of soldiers and art experts tasked with protecting and recovering looted art, were determined to stop the Nazis from escaping with France's cultural treasures. The Monuments Men worked tirelessly to track down stolen artworks, intercepting trains and convoys filled with priceless art as they fled towards Germany. Thanks to their efforts, many of the works looted by the Nazis were recovered and returned to France after the war.

One of the most dramatic moments in the Louvre's World War II story came in 1944, during the liberation of Paris. As the German army prepared to retreat, Hitler issued a series of orders known as the Nero Decree, which called for the destruction of Paris's cultural landmarks, including the Louvre. Hitler viewed the destruction of Paris as a way to demoralize the Allies and rob them of the city's symbolic and cultural importance. However, General Dietrich von Choltitz, the German military governor of Paris, famously refused to carry out Hitler's orders, sparing the city's monuments, including the Louvre, from destruction. Von Choltitz's defiance ensured that the Louvre and its remaining collection survived the war intact, though many of its treasures remained hidden in the countryside.

Following the liberation of Paris, one of the most pressing tasks for the Louvre's staff was the return of the evacuated artworks. This process was fraught with logistical challenges, as many of the artworks had been scattered across multiple locations, and some had been damaged during the war. Nevertheless, thanks to the meticulous records kept by Jaujard and his team, the vast majority of the Louvre's collection was eventually returned to the museum. In the years that followed, the Louvre became a symbol of France's resilience in the face of Nazi occupation, and the successful preservation of its art collection was seen as a triumph of French cultural identity.

The story of the Louvre during World War II also serves as a reminder of the broader efforts to protect art and cultural heritage during times of conflict. The Louvre was just one of many institutions across Europe that faced the threat of Nazi looting and destruction, and the efforts to safeguard art extended beyond France to other occupied countries, including Italy, Poland, and the Netherlands. In each of these countries, museum curators, art historians, and ordinary citizens took extraordinary risks to protect their cultural heritage, often at great personal cost. The story of the Louvre's wartime evacuation and the broader effort to protect art during World War II has since inspired numerous books, documentaries, and films, most notably the 2014 film *The Monuments Men*, which dramatizes the efforts of the Allied forces to recover looted art.

In the decades since the war, the Louvre has continued to play a central role in the ongoing efforts to recover art that was looted by the Nazis. Many of the works stolen from Jewish families and other victims of the Holocaust remain missing, and museums like the Louvre have worked closely with international organizations to track down and return these stolen works to their rightful owners. The Louvre has also participated in exhibitions and initiatives aimed at educating the public about the wartime looting of art and the importance of preserving cultural heritage in times of conflict.

In conclusion, the Louvre's role during World War II is a testament to the power of art and culture to endure even in the face of war and destruction. The efforts of Jacques Jaujard and his team to evacuate and protect the museum's collection were acts of heroism that helped preserve some of humanity's greatest artistic achievements. The Louvre, as both a symbol of French national identity and a treasure trove of world art, was at the center of the broader struggle to protect cultural heritage from the ravages of war. The successful preservation of its collection during World War II stands as a reminder of the importance of safeguarding our shared cultural heritage and the role that art plays in defining who we are as a people and as a civilization.

Chapter 19: Art Heists and Mysteries of the Louvre

The Louvre, with its vast collection of invaluable masterpieces, is not just the most visited museum in the world but also one of the most tantalizing targets for art thieves and a source of numerous art-related mysteries. Over the centuries, its halls have been the site of daring heists, mysterious disappearances, and enigmatic incidents that have left experts and art lovers puzzled. The tales of stolen art, unsolved mysteries, and hidden treasures connected to the Louvre continue to intrigue and fascinate, adding an extra layer of allure to the museum's already storied history.

One of the most famous and audacious art heists in history involved none other than the Louvre's most iconic piece: *Mona Lisa* by Leonardo da Vinci. The theft of this small but world-renowned painting in 1911 shocked not only France but the entire world. On the morning of August 21, 1911, the Louvre's staff realized that *Mona Lisa* was missing. The painting, usually displayed with minimal security, had been carefully removed from its frame, leaving behind an empty space where da Vinci's masterpiece had once hung. What made the theft even more confounding was the methodical precision with which it was carried out. The museum was closed for the day, and it appeared as though the painting had vanished without a trace, sparking a media frenzy and an international manhunt.

The theft was executed by an Italian man named Vincenzo Peruggia, who had been working at the Louvre as a handyman. His motivation was rooted in a sense of nationalism, as he believed that the painting, which had been brought to France by Leonardo da Vinci centuries earlier, rightfully belonged in Italy. Peruggia's plan was surprisingly simple: he hid inside the museum overnight and, once the building was quiet, he took the painting off the wall, concealed it under his work smock, and calmly walked out the next morning. Despite its simplicity, the theft caused global outrage. The Louvre was temporarily closed, and the public reacted with a mixture of disbelief and fury, not only at the audacity of the crime but also at the apparent ease with which it had been carried out. For two years, the whereabouts of the *Mona Lisa* remained a mystery. The painting's fame grew exponentially during this time, as newspapers around the world ran stories speculating on its fate.

In 1913, the mystery was finally solved when Peruggia tried to sell the painting to an art dealer in Florence, Italy. His attempt to return the *Mona Lisa* to its "rightful" home failed when the dealer alerted the authorities, leading to Peruggia's arrest and the recovery of the painting. The *Mona Lisa* was triumphantly returned to the Louvre, and while the painting had been relatively obscure prior to its theft, the global publicity surrounding the heist elevated it to legendary status. Today, *Mona Lisa* is the most famous painting in the world, and millions of visitors come to the Louvre each year to catch a glimpse of her mysterious smile, an enigma made even more captivating by the painting's dramatic history.

The *Mona Lisa* heist may be the most famous theft from the Louvre, but it is far from the only one. The museum has been the target of several other art thefts, some of which remain unsolved to this day. In the early 20th century, the Louvre experienced another high-profile theft when an Egyptian statue of *Sekhemka*, a beautifully carved limestone figure dating back to the 5th Dynasty of ancient Egypt, was stolen. Unlike the *Mona Lisa*, which was recovered, the *Sekhemka* statue vanished without a trace, and despite extensive efforts to track it down, it has never been found. The theft of the *Sekhemka* statue is one of the great unsolved art mysteries in the Louvre's history, leaving experts and investigators to speculate about its fate. Some believe it was stolen by private collectors, while others think it may have been smuggled out of France and sold on the black market.

One of the more bizarre art heist attempts in Louvre history occurred in 1976 when a group of thieves tried to steal a priceless Rembrandt painting from the museum. The painting, titled *Bathsheba at Her Bath*, was targeted by a criminal gang who believed they could sell it for millions of dollars. However, the thieves' plan went awry when they discovered that the painting was too large to fit through the Louvre's narrow doorways, forcing them to abandon the heist. While they managed to escape, the botched attempt was later used as evidence of the increased sophistication required to successfully steal artwork from a museum as heavily guarded as the Louvre.

Not all of the Louvre's art heists have involved grand-scale thefts. Some have been more subtle, involving the disappearance of smaller, lesser-known works that are often overlooked in the museum's vast collection. For example, in 1977, a small ivory carving from the medieval period was stolen from the museum. The thief, taking advantage of a momentary lapse in security, simply picked up the carving and walked out of the museum undetected. Despite its size, the carving was highly valuable, and its theft underscored the challenge of protecting the Louvre's enormous collection, which spans multiple floors and countless galleries.

Beyond thefts, the Louvre is also the subject of various art-related mysteries and legends. One of the most persistent legends surrounding the Louvre is that of hidden, undiscovered artworks that lie buried beneath the museum. The Louvre was originally built as a medieval fortress in the late 12th century, and over the centuries, various expansions, renovations, and reconstructions have taken place. Some believe that during these renovations, certain artworks or treasures may have been hidden or forgotten, lying beneath the museum's foundations, waiting to be rediscovered. While there is no concrete evidence to support this theory, it has captivated the imagination of historians and art enthusiasts alike.

One of the most famous mysteries associated with the Louvre involves the painting *The Wedding at Cana* by Paolo Veronese. This massive 16th-century masterpiece, which depicts the biblical wedding where Jesus turned water into wine, was looted by Napoleon Bonaparte's army during his campaigns in Italy. The painting was brought to France and hung in the Louvre, where it remains to this day. However, the painting's journey to the Louvre is shrouded in mystery. It is unclear how exactly the French managed to transport such a large painting from Italy to Paris, especially given the difficulties of moving a canvas of that size through the rugged terrain. The painting's original placement in the Louvre has also been a subject of debate, with some suggesting that it was hidden or misplaced for several years before finally being displayed in the museum's Grande Galerie.

Another enduring mystery surrounding the Louvre is connected to the museum's vast collection of ancient artifacts. The Louvre is home to one of the world's largest collections of ancient Egyptian, Greek, and Roman antiquities, many of which were acquired during the 19th and early 20th centuries. However, the provenance of some of these artifacts remains a mystery. While many were obtained through legitimate archaeological excavations, others were acquired through less transparent means, often during periods of colonial expansion. This has led to ongoing debates about the rightful ownership of certain artifacts in the Louvre's collection, with some countries calling for the return of culturally significant pieces that were taken during periods of imperial conquest. For example, Egypt has long requested the return of the *Dendera Zodiac*, a famous ancient Egyptian ceiling relief that was taken from the Temple of Hathor at Dendera and is now displayed in the Louvre. The debate over the repatriation of artifacts is a complex and contentious issue, with no easy resolution in sight, but it is a mystery that continues to hang over the Louvre's antiquities collection.

In addition to thefts and mysterious acquisitions, the Louvre has also been at the center of conspiracy theories and paranormal legends.

One such legend involves the Louvre's infamous glass pyramid, designed by architect I. M. Pei and completed in 1989. The pyramid, which serves as the main entrance to the museum, was initially met with controversy, as its modern design stood in stark contrast to the classical architecture of the surrounding palace. Over the years, the pyramid has become the subject of numerous conspiracy theories, with some speculating that its design is linked to secret societies such as the Freemasons or the Illuminati. These theories were popularized by Dan Brown's bestselling novel *The Da Vinci Code*, which used the Louvre as a central location in its story of hidden symbols, religious secrets, and ancient conspiracies. While there is no evidence to support these claims, they have added to the sense of mystery and intrigue that surrounds the Louvre.

The Louvre's role in art theft, mysteries, and legends is not just a reflection of its immense cultural significance but also a reminder of the complex relationship between art, history, and human desire. Throughout its long history, the museum has been a symbol of artistic achievement, a target for criminals, and a repository of untold stories waiting to be uncovered. Whether through the daring heist of the *Mona Lisa*, the disappearance of ancient artifacts, or the unresolved mysteries surrounding its vast collection, the Louvre remains a place where the line between history and legend is often blurred. Its art heists and mysteries have become part of its allure, inviting visitors not only to admire its masterpieces but also to ponder the secrets that may still lie within its walls.

As long as art continues to captivate the human imagination, the Louvre will remain a focal point for both appreciation and intrigue, serving as a testament to the enduring power of art to inspire, mystify, and challenge our understanding of the world. The Louvre's collection is not only a display of human creativity but also a reminder of the lengths people will go to possess, protect, and uncover the secrets behind these priceless works.

Chapter 20: The Louvre's Sculptures Garden

The Louvre's sculpture garden, known as the Cour Marly and Cour Puget, is one of the most enchanting and historically significant spaces within the museum. It's a place where visitors can step out of the confines of the indoor galleries and experience art in an airy, light-filled environment that evokes a connection between the sculptures and the natural world. The two courtyards are a tribute not only to the Louvre's unparalleled collection of French sculptures but also to the seamless blend of architecture and nature. With their high glass ceilings allowing natural light to flood the space, these sculpture gardens offer a tranquil retreat amid the museum's vast collections. They provide a unique atmosphere where art can be appreciated in a setting that feels open and contemplative, much like the gardens and royal parks in which many of these sculptures were originally displayed.

The history of the sculpture gardens is intertwined with the history of the Louvre itself. The Cour Marly and Cour Puget are relatively recent additions to the museum, but they house sculptures from earlier centuries, dating back to the reign of Louis XIV, the Sun King. In the 17th century, during Louis XIV's reign, the Louvre was primarily a royal palace, and many of the sculptures now in the gardens were originally created to adorn the gardens of the Château de Marly, a private royal retreat built by Louis XIV outside Paris. Marly was a place of luxury and splendor, where the king and his close circle could escape the rigid formality of Versailles and enjoy a more intimate and relaxed atmosphere. The sculptures commissioned for Marly were intended to reflect the themes of leisure, nature, and mythology, often portraying gods, goddesses, and mythical creatures in dynamic, expressive poses. These sculptures played an essential role in creating an idyllic, almost magical environment in Marly's gardens.

The Cour Marly, named after the Château de Marly, showcases many of these sculptures, transporting visitors back to the 17th-century world of Louis XIV's court. The Cour Marly's open and expansive layout allows visitors to view the sculptures from multiple angles, giving them a sense of the spatial relationships and visual drama that these works were originally intended to evoke when placed in outdoor settings. One of the most famous sculptures in the Cour Marly is *The Marly Horses* by Guillaume Coustou, an iconic representation of the French Baroque style. These monumental sculptures, completed in the early 18th century, depict two rearing horses being restrained by grooms, capturing a moment of intense physical struggle and movement. The dynamic poses of the horses, combined with the detailed rendering of their musculature and the grooms' efforts to control them, give the sculptures a sense of energy and vitality that still captivates viewers today.

Other notable works in the Cour Marly include *Neptune and Amphitrite* by Nicolas Coustou, a grand depiction of the sea god and his wife, embodying the mythological themes that were so popular in the art of Louis XIV's time. These sculptures were originally part of the elaborate fountains that adorned the gardens of Marly, and their presence in the Louvre's sculpture garden today offers a glimpse into the grandeur and opulence of royal garden design in the 17th and 18th centuries. The combination of mythological subject matter and the intricate craftsmanship of the sculptures creates a sense of timeless beauty, reminding visitors of the close relationship between art, nature, and power during Louis XIV's reign.

The Cour Puget, the counterpart to the Cour Marly, is named after the renowned French sculptor Pierre Puget, and it houses a collection of large-scale works from the 17th and 18th centuries. Like the Cour Marly, the Cour Puget is designed to evoke the feeling of being in a grand outdoor space, despite being enclosed by the Louvre's walls. The sculptures here were often created for royal gardens and public spaces, and their monumental scale reflects their intended purpose as focal points in expansive outdoor settings. One of the highlights of the Cour Puget is Puget's own masterpiece, *Milo of Croton*, a dramatic depiction of the ancient Greek athlete Milo as he is attacked by a lion. The sculpture captures the moment of intense physical struggle, with Milo's muscular body contorted as he fights off the beast. Puget's skill in rendering the human form in such a dynamic and emotionally charged pose made this sculpture one of the most celebrated works of its time.

Other important works in the Cour Puget include *Perseus and Andromeda* by Pierre Puget, which showcases the sculptor's ability to convey both beauty and heroism in his depiction of the mythological story. Perseus, the hero, is shown in a graceful and powerful stance as he rescues Andromeda, who is chained to a rock and awaiting her fate. The sculpture's composition, with its flowing lines and intricate details, reflects the Baroque style's emphasis on movement and emotional intensity. The inclusion of mythological themes in the Cour Puget, much like in the Cour Marly, highlights the way in which French sculptors of the 17th and 18th centuries drew inspiration from classical antiquity, imbuing their works with a sense of timelessness and grandeur.

The architectural design of the Cour Marly and Cour Puget plays a crucial role in enhancing the visitor's experience of the sculptures. The glass ceilings, designed by architect I. M. Pei as part of the Louvre's extensive renovations in the 1980s and 1990s, allow natural light to illuminate the sculptures, creating shifting patterns of light and shadow throughout the day. This natural illumination evokes the experience of viewing sculptures in an outdoor garden, where changing light conditions can alter the way a work of art is perceived. The vast, open spaces of the courtyards provide a sense of freedom and openness, contrasting with the more confined galleries elsewhere in the Louvre, and allowing visitors to fully appreciate the scale and detail of the sculptures. The combination of art, architecture, and natural light in these courtyards creates a contemplative and serene environment, encouraging visitors to slow down and engage more deeply with the artworks.

In addition to their historical significance, the sculptures in the Cour Marly and Cour Puget offer insight into the evolution of French sculpture during the 17th and 18th centuries. This period was marked by a shift in artistic priorities, as sculptors moved away from the rigid formalism of earlier styles and embraced a more expressive, dynamic approach to their work. The Baroque style, with its emphasis on movement, emotion, and dramatic contrasts, became the dominant aesthetic during this time, and many of the sculptures in the Louvre's gardens reflect this trend. The focus on mythological and allegorical subjects also reflects the broader cultural context of the period, in which art was seen as a means of communicating the ideals of the monarchy and the state. Many of the works in the Cour Marly and Cour Puget were commissioned by Louis XIV and his successors as a way of demonstrating the power and grandeur of the French monarchy, and they continue to serve as a testament to the enduring influence of royal patronage on French art.

The Cour Marly and Cour Puget also offer a unique opportunity to explore the relationship between sculpture and the natural world. Many of the sculptures in these courtyards were originally created for outdoor settings, and their placement in the Louvre's sculpture garden allows visitors to appreciate how they were intended to interact with their surroundings. The use of natural light, the spacious layout of the courtyards, and the presence of plant life in some areas all contribute to an atmosphere that evokes the gardens and parks where these sculptures once stood. This connection to nature is particularly important in understanding the role of sculpture in the 17th and 18th centuries, when gardens were seen as extensions of the royal palace, designed to reflect the power and order of the monarchy.

The Louvre's sculpture gardens are not only a celebration of French art but also a reflection of the broader European tradition of sculpture. The works on display in the Cour Marly and Cour Puget were part of a larger artistic movement that spanned the continent, with sculptors in France drawing inspiration from their counterparts in Italy, Spain, and the Netherlands. The influence of classical antiquity is also evident in many of the sculptures, particularly in their mythological subject matter and their emphasis on idealized human forms. This dialogue between French sculpture and the wider European artistic tradition is one of the key themes that visitors can explore in the Louvre's sculpture gardens, providing a deeper understanding of the ways in which art transcends national boundaries.

In conclusion, the Louvre's sculpture gardens, the Cour Marly and Cour Puget, offer visitors a unique and immersive experience of French sculpture from the 17th and 18th centuries. The combination of natural light, expansive spaces, and carefully curated artworks creates a tranquil and contemplative environment where visitors can engage with some of the most important sculptures in French art history. From the dynamic poses of *The Marly Horses* to the dramatic intensity of *Milo of Croton*, the sculptures in these gardens reflect the artistic ideals of their time, while also offering insight into the broader cultural and historical context of the period. Whether you are a seasoned art lover or a first-time visitor to the Louvre, the sculpture gardens provide a serene and captivating space to explore the beauty and power of sculpture in a setting that bridges the gap between the museum's indoor galleries and the natural world.

Epilogue

And so, our journey through the incredible Louvre comes to an end—but the wonders you've explored are just the beginning! You've discovered ancient treasures, learned the stories behind some of the world's most famous masterpieces, and uncovered the secrets of one of the greatest museums ever built.

The Louvre is more than just a building filled with art. It's a place where history, culture, and imagination come together, a treasure trove of human creativity that spans thousands of years. From the majestic *Winged Victory* to the mysterious *Mona Lisa*, you've glimpsed just a fraction of the countless wonders within its walls.

But the Louvre still has so much more to offer, and each visit reveals something new. Whether you've already had the chance to walk its grand halls or are dreaming of seeing it someday, remember that the museum is always there, waiting for curious minds like yours to explore it.

As you close this book, let the spirit of adventure stay with you. Keep asking questions, keep discovering, and keep imagining all the amazing things the world has to offer. After all, the Louvre is just one of many places filled with stories waiting to be told.

Until next time, happy exploring!

The End.